# ENGAGING UNBELIEF

A Captivating
Strategy
from Augustine
& Aquinas

## CURTIS CHANG

InterVarsity Press
Downers Grove, Illinois

*InterVarsity Press, USA*
*P.O. Box 1400, Downers Grove, IL 60515-1426, USA*
*World Wide Web: www.ivpress.com*
*E-mail: mail@ivpress.com*

*Inter-Varsity Press, England*
*38 De Montfort Street, Leicester LE1 7GP, England*

*InterVarsity Press®, U.S.A., is the book-publishing division of InterVarsity Christian Fellowship/USA®, a student movement active on campus at hundreds of universities, colleges and schools of nursing in the United States of America, and a member movement of the International Fellowship of Evangelical Students. For information about local and regional activities, write Public Relations Dept., InterVarsity Christian Fellowship/USA, 6400 Schroeder Rd., P.O. Box 7895, Madison, WI 53707-7895.*

*Inter-Varsity Press, England, is the book-publishing division of the Universities and Colleges Christian Fellowship (formerly the Inter-Varsity Fellowship), a student movement linking Christian Unions in universities and colleges throughout the United Kingdom and the Republic of Ireland, and a member movement of the International Fellowship of Evangelical Students. For information about local and national activities write to UCCF, 38 De Montfort Street, Leicester LE1 7GP.*

*Cover photographs: Saint Thomas, Alinari/Art Resource, N.Y.; Saint Augustine, Erich Lessing/Art Resource, N.Y*

*USA ISBN 0-8308-2266-6*

*UK ISBN 0-85111-472-5*

*Printed in the United States of America ∞*

Library of Congress Cataloging-in-Publication Data

*Chang, Curtis, 1968-*
   *Engaging unbelief : a captivating strategy from Augustine & Aquinas / Curtis Chang*
      *p. cm.*
   *Includes bibliographical references.*
   *ISBN 0-8308-2266-6 (pbk. : alk. paper)*
      *1. Apologetics—History. 2. Augustine, Saint, Bishop of Hippo. De civitate Dei 3*
   *Thomas, Aquinas, Saint, 1225?-1274. Summa contra gentiles. I. Title.*


   *BT1109 .C46 2000*
   *239—dc21*
                                                                                          *00-040945*

British Library Cataloguing in Publication Data
*A catalogue record for this book is available from the British Library.*

20  19  18  17  16  15  14  13  12  11  10  9  8  7  6  5  4  3  2  1
16  15  14  13  12  11  10  09  08  07  06  05  04  03  02  01  00

To BaBa,
*who passed on to me*
*a love of history,*
*and MaMa,*
*who passed on to me*
*my first knowledge of God*

献给最初启蒙我于上帝的妈，
献给最初给予我对历史的爱的爸，

张忠恕

# Contents

# Preface

This book is an attempt to correspond with Augustine and Aquinas about the challenges facing Christians in the postmodern epoch. Like us, Augustine and Aquinas faced questions such as what to proclaim to a society that previously understood itself to be "Christian" but now seems to be fragmenting, and what to say when truths previously held to be universal are under assault from a disorienting religious pluralism. This book rests on the conviction that as a church sustained by God for two millennia now, we need not look upon the postmodern challenge as completely unprecedented. Rather, we must continually renew our relationship with our intellectual ancestors, as through them God desires to pass on much-needed wisdom.

Through many hours working on this project, I have gained an even more personal appreciation for Augustine and Aquinas. Both are stunning for the sheer brilliance and breadth of their writing, but they are also amazing for having composed their most significant treatises while engaging in full-time ministry. Aquinas traveled thousands of miles by foot to carry out the mission of his Dominican monastic order. Augustine daily faced the endless responsibilities of a bishop overseeing a regional ministry.

While my own writing and ministry are far more modest, I can imagine why Augustine and Aquinas insisted on combining these two pursuits. I serve as an area director of InterVarsity Christian Fellowship's ministry in Boston. While at times the demands of ministering to college students and supervising other campus ministers have threatened to overwhelm my scholarly efforts, the ongoing experience of campus ministry has enormously sharpened my writing. One cannot walk daily on the campuses of Harvard, MIT and Tufts—influential places that prefigure where our society is heading—and deny that a new epoch is emerging before our eyes. And one cannot work as a Christian missionary at these places without asking the question that lies at the heart of this book: How do we communicate the gospel to the people of this postmodern epoch?

Many colleagues, teachers and students have helped me reflect on this question. In some ways this book began during a summer of reading John Milbank's *Theology and Social Theory* with Timothy Shah. While Tim was pursuing his Ph.D. in political philosophy at Harvard and I was beginning my ministry, Tim served as my intellectual "pusher," feeding my addiction for great books. It was Tim who first suggested Aquinas's *Summa contra Gentiles* for my study. This project took further form as an independent study supervised by Gwenfair Walters, professor of church history at Gordon-Conwell Theological Seminary. Her willingness to allow me to tackle an almost ridiculously ambitious project allowed me to get started; her advice and encouragement have kept me going. Others who read various drafts and offered helpful feedback include Vinay Samuel, Robert Sweetman, John Velz, Brian Walsh and Lisa Lamb.

Another great benefit of my mission to college students is the privilege of belonging to a larger movement of fellow missionaries. Like the Dominicans in Aquinas's day, InterVarsity Christian Fellowship is a relatively young "order" of remarkable people who have forsaken more lucrative endeavors to dedicate themselves to missions (and who, like the original mendicant movements, have to raise their own financial support!). That my manuscript actually made it to publication is due in no small part to Bob Fryling, publisher of InterVarsity Press. He took this first-time author seriously and has served as a crucial advocate for me in many ways. Thanks also go to my editor at the Press, Gary Deddo; it is a rare treat to have my former professor also serve as my editor, but doubly so when that person has been as influential in my theological education as Gary has been. I am also indebted to my friend and colleague in Boston, Andy Crouch, who offered invaluable critiques and suggestions. I especially wish to thank the hundreds of students who have passed through my life with InterVarsity. They are too many to cite by name, but their very real struggles and triumphs, questions and beliefs animate the pages that follow.

Finally, my deepest gratitude and appreciation go to my wife, Jody. In our ministry with InterVarsity, she has been my best partner in responding to our epoch. In my writing, she has been my most careful and faithful editor by far. Her very presence in my life reminds me that in this book and in everything else, I have received blessings from God far beyond what I deserve.

# 1

# Epochal Challenges

NORTH AFRICA, 413. THE FAMOUS BISHOP opened the letter to find yet another request.[1] Once again someone was asking him to write a book. A renowned man of letters, Augustine was used to requests from agents seeking new literature or people desiring his views on all sorts of topics. As a busy bishop concerned with the many practical details of leading the North African church, he was also used to dismissing such requests with grouchy replies like "I wish I could snatch you away from your titillating disquisitions and ram you into the sort of cares I have to cope with."[2] Yet this particular request drew his attention.

The letter was from Marcellinus, Augustine's lay disciple and close friend. Marcellinus had been sent to seek the Roman imperial government's assistance to resolve the dispute between Catholics and Donatists in North Africa—a persistent source of headaches for Augustine. But Marcellinus's urgent request had to do with a different concern. He had sought to convert Volusianus, the Roman proconsul to Africa, to the Christian faith. Volusianus came from a noble Roman family, steeped in classical pagan culture. He headed a social group of educated, sophisticated Romans to whom, as one historian noted, "Christianity appeared, as it appears to

---

[1]All dates are A.D. unless otherwise noted.
[2]Quoted in Peter Brown, *Augustine of Hippo* (Berkeley: University of California Press, 1969), p. 299.

many today, as a religion out of joint with the natural assumptions of a whole culture."[3]

Marcellinus needed help. He reported that Volusianus showed some interest but had mounted several strong objections. Among his strongest was the accusation that the rise of Christianity had caused the pressing ills now afflicting the Roman Empire. Volusianus had in mind, of course, the horrific and still inconceivable events of three years earlier. For three days in August 410 a Gothic army led by Alaric had captured Rome, sacked it and burned parts of the city to the ground. In the preceding eight hundred years Rome had never fallen into enemy hands, and to many it seemed as if an entire society was disintegrating. Volusianus's impulse to pin the blame on Christianity was shared by many of his peers. So Marcellinus asked Augustine to write a work that would help him answer such accusations.[4]

Augustine the intellectual was well aware that this educated class of pagan challengers could define the dominant perspective of Roman culture. His own past in precisely that circle had taught him that this intelligentsia could easily seize events like the sack of Rome and produce a widely accepted interpretation that would "harden a prestigious tradition against the spread of Christianity."[5]

Augustine the pastor also knew firsthand that Rome's seeming collapse already had rocked the Christian world. Almost a century earlier to the year, Constantine had undergone his famous conversion which linked the Empire with Christianity, a linkage that had grown so tight in the ensuing years that leading Christians had come to regard Christian and Roman civilization as coterminous.[6] For the church, therefore, the fall of Rome felt like a blow to its own solar plexus. St. Jerome was so shaken that he complained he could not dictate his commentary on Ezekiel;

---

[3]Ibid., p. 301.

[4]See footnote 1 in Augustine, *City of God*, trans. Henry Bettenson (London: Penguin, 1987), p. 5; see also John O'Meara's introduction to ibid., pp. x-xi. In subsequent citations from *City of God* (hereafter *COG*) I will use the classic book and chapter designations but also include page numbers from this Penguin edition. All quotations are from the Penguin edition.

[5]Brown, *Augustine of Hippo*, p. 302.

[6]Robert Markus, *Saeculum* (London: Cambridge University Press, 1970), pp. 28-39.

indeed he could not remember his own name or do anything but remain silent. "If Rome can perish," he wrote, "what can be safe?"[7] Asking this and similar questions, anxious and confused Christian refugees from Rome had streamed into Augustine's congregations in North Africa.[8]

Thus Marcellinus's request no doubt rang in Augustine's mind as the representative note of challenges and concerns echoing through the era. As he set aside the letter, ideas that had emerged in his letters and sermons over the past few years began to coalesce; soon they took shape in the beginnings of a singular, monumental work: *City of God*.[9] The year Augustine received the request, he would preface book 1 thus: "Here, my dear Marcellinus, is the fulfillment of my promise, a book in which I have taken upon myself the task of defending the glorious City of God against those who prefer their own gods to the Founder of that City."[10] Thirteen years and twenty-one books later, the perpetually harried bishop would recall the original request behind *City of God:* "And now, as I think," he wrote in its last lines, "I have discharged my debt, with the completion by God's help, of this huge work."[11] "This huge work" would stand as one of Augustine's most lasting contributions to Christianity, then and now.

*A Dominican priory in Naples, 1259.* About eight hundred years later, another thinker of the church opened a letter from an evangelist requesting help.[12] It was a rather unexpected request, for while Thomas Aquinas

---

[7]O'Meara, introduction to *COG*, p. x.

[8]James J. O'Donnell, *Augustine* (Boston: Twayne, 1985), p. 11.

[9]O'Meara, introduction to *COG*, p. xiv.

[10]Augustine, preface to *COG* 1, p. 5.

[11]*COG* 22.30, p. 1091.

[12]The date is not exact, but many scholars concur on this rough date as the beginning of *Summa contra Gentiles*. On the question see John Finnis, *Aquinas* (Oxford: Oxford University Press, 1998), p. xix. On the location of Aquinas at this time, see Norman Kretzmann, "Thomas Aquinas," in *Routledge Encyclopedia of Philosophy* (London: Routledge, 1998), 1:329. Kretzmann believes Aquinas may have originally started the work in Paris but soon moved to Naples, while others place him in Naples from the beginning. No one is able to marshal absolutely convincing evidence either way. See also Anton C. Pegis, introduction to *Summa contra Gentiles*, bk. 1, trans. Anton C. Pegis (Notre Dame, Ind.: University of Notre Dame Press, 1975), pp. 15-17. As with *City of God*, in citing *Summa contra Gentiles* (hereafter *SCG*) I will use classic book, chapter and paragraph references as well as page numbers from the University of Notre Dame edition.

had already gained a reputation as a leading authority, it was hardly on matters that seemed immediately relevant to those in the mission field. Most of his works had been commentaries on authors long dead or on rather technical questions of philosophy.[13] Indeed, Aquinas often appeared to prefer to dwell in an abstract realm, ignoring the contemporary world. One anecdote recalls Aquinas making an obligatory appearance at a court dinner of King Louis IX. The customary exchange of political news and gossip filled the dinner-table conversation. Aquinas remained silent, only occasionally nodding politely to guests next to him. Suddenly, in the middle of the dinner, he slammed his heavy fist (for he was a very large man) on the table with a thud that silenced conversation. As all eyes turned to him in shock, he cried out with the satisfaction of one who has just solved a preoccupying problem, "And *that* will settle the Manichees!"[14]

The letter now before him was not asking him to respond to an ancient school of philosophy like Manichaeism. Nevertheless, it captured his attention. Its author was Ramon of Penyaforte, who was, like Aquinas, a Dominican monk. Ramon had pioneered missions to the Muslims in Spain, even establishing Dominican schools where friars could receive training on evangelizing this population. He was on the cutting edge of the development of missions as an alternative to the crusades. Yet for all his efforts, Ramon had few results to show.[15] He was now writing to ask Aquinas, according to one fourteenth-century chronicle, "to compose a work against the errors of unbelievers, by which both the cloud of darkness might be dispelled and the teaching of the true Sun might be made manifest to those who refuse to believe."[16]

Ramon of Penyaforte's failure in Spain was simply one fault line of Western Christianity's relatively recent encounter with Islam—Christian-

---

[13]See Pegis, introduction to *SCG* 1, pp. 16-17.

[14]G. K. Chesterton, *Saint Thomas Aquinas: The Dumb Ox* (New York: Doubleday, 1956), pp. 97-101.

[15]Benjamin Z. Kedar, *Crusade and Mission* (Princeton, N.J.: Princeton University Press, 1984), pp. 137, 143-44.

[16]James Waltz, "Muhammad and the Muslims in St. Thomas Aquinas," *The Muslim World* 66 (April 1976): 82 n. 3. On the academic debate over this account of the *Summa contra Gentiles*'s origins, see the appendix.

ity's first experience with another unified faith that like itself claimed universal status and unique truth. Even the paganism of Augustine's day claimed authority only for its own particular society. In a shockingly brief time a new and self-confident religion had erupted to surround Christendom. From the west via Spain, the south via North Africa and the whole Near East, Islam confronted Christianity. Little wonder then that Ramon's monks experienced great difficulty in getting Islamic audiences to believe or even listen to their claim that Christianity was a superior religion. Like no other challenger, Islam could rub against Christianity with the massive solidity and resistance of a tectonic plate. The crusades were but the most obvious example of how the seismic challenge of Islam disturbed Christianity and defined the medieval era.

Even before Ramon's letter Thomas Aquinas had registered other tremors from this encounter with Islam. In particular, he was sensitive to developments based in Spain. The Islamic philosophers in Spain had brought the works of Aristotle—long lost to the West—to the attention of Aquinas and other Christian intellectuals. In the previous century alone numerous Islamic commentaries on Aristotle had suddenly descended on the West. Like the Islamic society that bore it to the West, this seemingly complete, self-sufficient and foreign body of knowledge threatened the worldview then dominant in Christendom. In his own efforts to understand and respond to Aristotle, Aquinas had witnessed firsthand how this intellectual invasion disrupted the Christian world. Only four decades earlier the University of Paris (which granted Aquinas his license to teach) had received a ruling from a provincial synod prohibiting the reading of Aristotle's works on natural philosophy "on pain of excommunication."[17] During Aquinas's own time at the university, a bitter debate over the study of Aristotle had resolved itself in favor of the study of that philosopher only by the narrowest of margins.

As Aquinas set down Ramon's letter his ever-active mind began to conceive the shape of his response. He was concerned to meet the Span-

---

[17]Jan A. Aertsen, "Aquinas's Philosophy in Its Historical Setting," in *The Cambridge Companion to Aquinas*, ed. Norman Kretzmann and Eleonore Stump (Cambridge: Cambridge University Press, 1993), p. 20. For correlation with Aquinas's own timeline, see Pegis, introduction to *SCG* 1, pp. 15-17.

ish monks' practical needs, but those needs also triggered broader, deeper and more abstract motions in his thought. Over the next five years he would fashion those intellectual motions into one enormous work of four books. One eminent Thomist scholar notes the "keen personal initiative" that fills the pages of this work: *Summa contra Gentiles*, arguably the greatest work that this giant of a thinker ever completed.[18]

### The Postmodern Challenge

Church history is best practiced as an exercise in correspondence. The historian sends inquiries out into the murky past, seeking to understand our ancestors in all their unique historical particularities. Yet it is a tenet of postmodernism that every historian inevitably inquires not as a dispassionate, objective observer but always as one bearing some contemporary agenda, albeit often undeclared.

Christian church historians have their agenda already declared for them by Scripture. The book of Hebrews enjoins the church to pay attention to that "great cloud of witnesses; communion with our ancestors is meant to encourage those of us facing the next challenge in "the race marked out for us" (Heb 12:1 NIV). As Augustine described his own agenda in researching the apostolic tradition, the church historian seeks to "carve a channel from them to our own times."[19]

In this book, then, I seek to correspond with two monumental members of that "cloud of witnesses" through their seminal works. I read Augustine's *City of God* and Aquinas's *Summa contra Gentiles* to understand these works in their own historical terms, but I also unapologetically pose questions dictated by the challenges confronting the church today. And I expect that our ancestors will answer if we pay attention.

The topic of my correspondence is the particular kind of challenge that looms before the church today: what I term an "epochal challenge." An epochal challenge is a development that fundamentally threatens how the church has traveled the most recent leg of its journey. While there is

---

[18]*Summa Theologica*, by which Aquinas is more popularly recognized, was never fully completed. For the personal nature of *SCG*, see the comments of M. D. Chenu, *Introduction à l'étude de saint Thomas d'Aquin* (Paris: J. Vrin, 1950), p. 247

[19]Quoted in Markus, *Saeculum*, p. xxiii.

no precise criterion for what qualifies as an epochal challenge, Christians encountering one feel that the ground they have taken for granted is shifting. The basic reference points that have guided how they inhabit their epoch as Christians seem to be toppling. To use some popular terms, an epochal challenge presents "paradigm shifts" or new "worldviews" that feel disorienting to the church.

Observers of our culture—whether Christians or not—widely note that we face a massive paradigm shift called *postmodernity*. Redescribing postmodernity is certainly not my goal here; suffice it to say that we are in the midst of an emerging new era. One analyst has thus summarized the multiple forces behind postmodernity:

> Western culture is in the middle of a fundamental transformation; a "shape of life" is growing old. The demise of the old is being hastened by the end of colonialism, the uprising of women, the revolt of other cultures against white Western hegemony, shifts in the balance of economic and political power within the world economy, and a growing awareness of the costs as well as the benefits of scientific and technological "progress."[20]

All these forces of change have fostered a suspicion that the hegemony of Western modernity marginalized those whom postmodern critics describe as the "other" or the "different." Since modernity excluded the marginal by upholding its own norms and truths—often under the guise of a universal rationality—postmodernity now challenges all norms and truths. Thus postmodernity conceives of religion as radically relative, depicts history as a Nietzschean record of the raw will to power and exercises a general hermeneutic of suspicion toward all literature.

While this epochal challenge affects the wider culture, postmodernity particularly threatens many paradigms that have long guided the church. For instance, religious relativism undermines the church's long-held claim to universal truth. The fragmentation of Western culture splits Christianity's historical alliance with that culture, while also giving rise to histories that implicate Christianity in a wide range of the culture's ills—

---

[20]Jane Flax, quoted in J. Richard Middleton and Brian J. Walsh, *Truth Is Stranger Than It Used to Be* (Downers Grove, Ill.: InterVarsity Press, 1995), p. 24.

racial conflicts, the ecological crisis, battles over sexuality and gender.
Biblical scholars influenced by postmodern literary theories now scan
Scripture not for God's revelation but for evidence of socioeconomic and
political agendas.[21] It is no surprise that the average Christian looks out at
the changes swirling within our culture and sighs, as one writer put it,
"Toto, I don't think we're in Kansas anymore."[22]

### The Outbreak of Conflict in Epochal Challenges

Instead, the church finds it has landed in a state of conflict. Escalating
conflict between the church and the rest of society is a frequent symptom
of an epochal challenge. Each epoch usually establishes particular terms
of peaceful coexistence between church and society. Where disputes do
arise, there exist commonly acknowledged authorities to resolve or at
least restrict the tension. The medieval European and Byzantine epochs
of Christendom stand as the most obvious examples of a particularly
close partnership.

An epochal challenge tends to erode the terms of such partnerships.
Each partnership is constructed under a particular worldview; the emer-
gence of a new worldview undermines the established harmony. The old
sources of authority are no longer shared by all. For instance, the epochal
challenge of the Reformation fragmented the medieval consensus
regarding the authority of the Catholic Church over all Europe and
unleashed a string of religious wars. This conflict marked the transition
to the modern epoch, as the Enlightenment self-consciously sought to
find new terms for peaceful coexistence between society and religion.

---

[21]For examples, see Terrence Tilly, *Postmodern Theologies: Challenges of Religious Diversity*
(Maryknoll, N.Y.: Orbis, 1995), on the effect of religious pluralism. See Forrest G. Wood,
*The Arrogance of Faith: Christianity and Race in America from the Colonial Era to the
Twentieth Century* (New York: Alfred A. Knopf, 1990), as an example of the attempt to
implicate Christianity in the history of American racism. For the environmental movement's attempt to blame the ecological crisis on Christianity's historical impact, see Tony
Campolo, *How to Rescue the Earth Without Worshiping Nature* (Nashville: Thomas Nelson,
1992), chap. 2. For an example of the postmodern suspicion in literary criticism, see
Jacques Derrida, *Speech and Phenomena*, trans. David Allison (Evanston, Ill.: Northwestern University Press, 1972). For its specific application to the Bible, see Juan Luis Seg-
undo, *Theology of Liberation*, trans. John Drury (Maryknoll, N.Y.: Orbis, 1976).
[22]Andy Crouch, "Not in Kansas," *Re:Generation Quarterly* 2, no. 2 (Summer 1996): 41-42.

The West increasingly turned to modern liberalism as the new authority. This authority would demarcate the realm of public facts from that of private values, assigning the former to secular society and the latter to religion.[23]

In the twilight of modernity, these pacts feel increasingly tenuous. The intractable conflicts surrounding abortion, homosexuality and the death penalty illustrate the breakdown of modernity's neat demarcation between public facts and private values. Alasdair MacIntyre describes such conflicts as being marked by "extreme *incommensurability* and *untranslatability*": worldviews facing off without any shared authority to adjudicate the dialogue, without even any shared language to use.[24] The incommensurability and untranslatability are especially pronounced given that postmodernity, while seeking to shatter modernity's governing conventions, has yet to offer any substantial replacements, especially for how religion fits with the rest of society. So in our fragmented age new conflicts have erupted between Christians and secular society, and the two parties struggle to find any common ground.

With more and more points of tension and fewer and fewer words to share, the former partners are sorely tempted to break off all negotiations and prepare for war. Only force, it appears to both, can resolve the conflict. In his 1991 book *Culture Wars*, political sociologist James Davison Hunter explored how evangelical Christians and secular society were headed for a clash as each sought to wield political power over the other. Three years later he revisited the scarred political landscape with an even more somber book: *Before the Shooting Begins.*[25] While the culture war has still been mostly restricted to political and cultural weapons, murders of abortion doctors by self-proclaimed Christians indicate that real shoot-

---

[23]Lesslie Newbigin, *Foolishness to the Greeks* (Grand Rapids, Mich.: Eerdmans, 1986), pp. 15-18. For an excellent discussion of how the post-Reformation religious conflict motivated a key figure in the development of modern liberalism, see Timothy Shah, *Hugo Grotius*, Ph.D. diss., Harvard University, 1999, chap. 2.

[24]Alasdair MacIntyre, *Three Rival Versions of Moral Enquiry* (Notre Dame, Ind.: University of Notre Dame Press, 1990), p. 4.

[25]James Davison Hunter, *Culture Wars* (New York: BasicBooks, 1991); and *Before the Shooting Begins* (New York: Free Press, 1994).

ing with live ammunition has already begun.[26]

Beyond the postindustrial West the commencement of hostilities is even more obvious: social pacts for managing religious tension have collapsed even more abruptly. As I write, today's newspaper headlines bear the violent signs of these times. In Rwanda and other African countries, the tattered curtains of colonialism that previously covered over deep hostilities have been slashed apart completely by the machetes of tribes bent on massacre. In the former Yugoslavia the sudden disintegration of communist regimes has released a wave of ethnic cleansing. And in Asian countries like Indonesia and Malaysia, modernity's golden promise of economic development for all has suffered currency meltdowns, triggering mob violence between disgruntled communities. In all these conflicts and still more that daily fill media reports, Christians, Muslims and Hindus figure prominently in the lists of combatants.

### The Need for a New Rhetorical Strategy

Given that conflict is an unavoidable reality of the current epochal challenge, the Christian is confronted with a dilemma. Unless the person wants to break off all contact with the rest of society, he or she must step forward and meet challengers face to face. And unless the Christian wants to overpower rivals by sheer force—either that of votes or of bullets—then he or she must at the very least figure out a way to speak. But what should be said?

The right words do not seem readily accessible. I discovered this early on in my work as a campus minister, in encounters with two students, Jake and Alex.[27] At Harvard University I befriended Jake, an extremely bright student from Montana. Jake is a Native American, but having been adopted by white parents at an early age, he knew little about that aspect of his past. He had come to believe in Christianity as a teenager through reading Hal Lindsey, an author who specialized in correlating biblical prophecies with historical events. By the time I met him, he had

---

[26]A chilling description of how Christian communities are increasingly contemplating violence in the antiabortion campaign can be found in the murder case of Dr. Barnett Slepian. See David Samuels, "Anti-abortion Odyssey," *New York Times Magazine*, March 21, 1999, pp. 47-93.

[27]Their names have been changed.

moved on to the works of Francis Schaeffer and other modern Christian philosophers. In my times with Jake, he would frequently try out various arguments that demonstrated the rationality of Christianity. He was mesmerized by the hope of working out an airtight case that would win over his non-Christian classmates.

I eventually said farewell to Jake when I left Boston for a year of missions in South Africa. During that year I received a letter with a Native American reservation as its return address. Jake was writing to inform me that he no longer could consider himself a Christian. He had been uncovering his Native American identity: he had found his original family and had changed his last name back to theirs. He had even left Boston to move in with this newfound family. The more time he spent with his people—especially those who practiced tribal religions—the less comfortable he felt with Christianity. Christianity and Christians, he explained, had almost obliterated his true people and his true self. How could he cling to this alien faith?

I confess I did not write back for months. Each time I tried, I could only stare at my stationery, not knowing how to fill its blank space.

I met Alex during an evangelistic presentation in a dorm at Clark University. A speaker had just outlined the historical evidence for Jesus and his resurrection. Alex stood in the back, his arms crossed and a bemused smile on his face. When I approached him and asked what he thought about the presentation, he shrugged and replied, "I don't see how you can know that any of this is true."

Eager to use all the apologetics training I had received, I proceeded to debate with him the historical evidence and reasoning involved. After an hour of lengthy debate, I thought I had maneuvered him into admitting a critical inconsistency in his logic. All my apologetics textbooks assured me that this represented a decisive accomplishment. Surely I had "won" a significant battle!

Alex contemplated his inconsistency for a moment, shrugged and replied, "Yeah, well, so what?"

"So what?" I responded in exasperation. "But . . . but . . . what you believe can't be true if you contradict yourself!"

Alex flashed another bemused smile, "But so what? Who's to say that your logic isn't just all made up? Who's to say that *everything* isn't just made up?" And with that he shrugged again, while in my befuddlement and frustration I could only lapse into silence. What was my next line supposed to be?

An epochal challenge is so challenging precisely because it presents problems fundamentally different from the previous epoch. The church's evangelists and apologists suddenly discover that the lines they've been taught have the feel of the Maginot Line, that elaborate fortress the French built on their borders after the trench warfare of World War I—only to discover in the new mobile warfare of World War II that German tanks could circle right around their defenses.

Postmodernity renders obsolete much of the rhetorical strategy we inherited from modernity. The one who demands an answer is not so often the philosophical atheist, but a Jake who asserts that Western Christianity has brutally marginalized native peoples. The challenger is not the aggressive secular humanist who attacks the rationality of Christianity, but an Alex who holds to a personally constructed epistemology of radical doubt. The old arguments no longer sway; the old spells no longer enchant.

### The Need for History in an Epochal Challenge

In recent years Christian thinkers have published books that seek to write the church some new lines.[28] Some of them are quite good and helpful. Indeed, I have wondered about my own wisdom in trying to add yet another book to this ever-growing collection. But it is essential to draw on church history as we seek to respond to contemporary questions. Many existing treatments of the postmodern challenge manifest a certain ahistorical tendency, as if this latest epochal challenge represents some threat unprecedented in the annals of Western Christianity. One writer has warned: "Apologetics is especially needed today, when the world stands at a triple crossroads and crisis. Western civilization is *for the first time in its history* in danger of dying. The reason is spiritual.

---

[28]See, for example, Timothy R. Phillips and Dennis L. Okholm, eds., *Christian Apologetics in the Postmodern World* (Downers Grove, Ill.: InterVarsity Press, 1995), or Anthony Thistleton, *Interpreting God and the Postmodern Self* (Grand Rapids, Mich.: Eerdmans, 1995).

It is losing its life, its soul; that soul was the Christian faith."[29]

This feeling that we are encountering an utterly unique threat, of course, imbues an epochal challenge with its disconcerting power. And that is why at such a "crossroads and crisis" we especially need to correspond with our cloud of witnesses. Because the truth is that this is not the first time Christianity has needed to figure out what to say when the Western civilization it is attached to seems to be in danger of dying. Augustine awaits our inquiries. Nor is today the first day that Christian evangelists sought the right words to address a rival civilization that emerged suddenly from the margins, animated by a different faith. Aquinas stands ready to reply.

### Taking Every Thought Captive

While the challenges faced by Augustine and Aquinas do correspond to the postmodern challenge in some key features, we must be wary of straight connections. It obviously would be foolish to enlist Augustine's actual arguments in *City of God* to respond to today's "pagan critics" or to believe that *Summa contra Gentiles* can serve as a textbook for evangelism to Muslims now living in Spain. I am also skeptical of the approach commonly found in attempts to popularize and update classic works, whereby the particular concerns of a classic work are systematized and then dogmatically applied to contemporary issues. Such an approach would argue, for instance, "If only more people would hold Augustine's position on sexuality, then our problem with abortion would be solved."

Historical epochs are simply too dissimilar for such direct appropriation. Corresponding with great thinkers of the past must involve reading beyond their positions to discern *how* and *why* they came to form those particular positions.

What I hope to accomplish is to discern the underlying rhetorical strategy behind Augustine's and Aquinas's responses. My thesis is that both *City of God* and *Summa contra Gentiles*, although very different works written by very different men in very different epochs, have a basi-

---

[29]Peter Kreeft and Ronald K. Tacelli, *Handbook of Christian Apologetics* (Downers Grove, Ill.: InterVarsity Press, 1994), p. 23, emphasis mine.

cally similar purpose and plan. The underlying strategy is what I label, borrowing St. Paul's terms, "taking every thought captive to obey Christ" (2 Cor 10:5). This rhetorical strategy involves three main components:

1. *entering* the challenger's story
2. *retelling* the story
3. *capturing* that retold tale within the gospel metanarrative

These three components will organize my discussion of both *City of God* and *Summa contra Gentiles*, so they merit some further introduction.

By entering the challenger's story, I mean that both authors initially operate within the challenger's worldview. At this stage, both seek a meeting based on the opponent's own paradigms and authorities. In seeking the most appropriate meeting place and sorting through all the different possibilities, Augustine and Aquinas are of course implicitly guided by the gospel. But since the meeting occurs within the challenger's story, Augustine and Aquinas will voluntarily restrict their explicit rhetoric to the challenger's own language. Neither will simply try to outshout the challenger from a self-enclosed Christian worldview or appeal to terms that the challenger does not share. Instead they will attempt to speak as fellow indwellers of a shared story.

Having entered the challenger's story, Augustine and Aquinas then retell the story from the inside. They reinterpret the challenger, again by appealing to the challenger's own terms. In fact, they will argue that their rendition is the truer one by the challenger's own standards. While Augustine and Aquinas still restrict themselves to the challenger's language at this stage, their intent is to reveal the incompleteness of the challenger's story. Thus they carefully rework the challenger's story in order to highlight its "tragic flaw." This flaw is tragic in the true Aristotelian sense: a weakness intrinsic to one's very nature that will inevitably lead to downfall. Like the great Greek tragedians, Augustine and Aquinas retell the story in a way that will intensify the dramatic tension of the tragic flaw and display its consequences to all. In doing so, they seek to prepare the audience for the necessary third stage.

Finally, Augustine and Aquinas capture this retold tale. Here they move beyond the terms of the challenger and tell their own story. Their story takes the form of a metanarrative: an overarching story that incorporates and explains all other stories within its own meaning. Their metanarrative is, of course, the gospel. Or to put it more precisely, they tell a specific version of the gospel metanarrative. Augustine and Aquinas handcraft their versions of the gospel metanarrative to take in the retold shape of the challenger's tale. Like sanded pegs falling into the holes of a massive woodwork, all the reworked aspects of the challenger's story—whether they are the desires of its characters, the flow of its plot or the direction of its dramatic action—now find their final and true place in the gospel.

The ability of the gospel metanarrative to take in all rival stories depends especially on its ability to "resolve" those stories. N. T. Wright, J. Richard Middleton and Brian Walsh have in various ways introduced the understanding that stories can get stuck in some plot tension and thus feel unresolved to those who listen.[30] For instance, if Jesus had broken off his parable of the prodigal son with the younger son in a far-off country enjoying his dissolute life with his father's riches, listeners would demand the next chapter. If Jesus did not know how to continue the story, the plot would have felt unsatisfying and unresolved.

Augustine and Aquinas will show how the challenger's story breaks down at the point of greatest tragic tension. In their rhetorical step of "capture," both will show that the tragic tension of the challenger's story—a tension they deliberately intensify—can be resolved only in the gospel.

### Epochal Challenges and "Story"

Clearly the concept of *story* is crucial to my understanding of the strategy Augustine and Aquinas pursue. Before I proceed, it will be helpful to clarify this concept and explain its significance in the postmodern epoch.

All human beings depend on story to live. As individuals, we need some narrative to organize our understanding of what otherwise would be

---

[30]N. T. Wright, "Jesus as the World's True Light," address delivered at InterVarsity Christian Fellowship's National Graduate Conference, January 2, 1999; Middleton and Walsh, *Truth Is Stranger*, pp. 181-83.

a chaotic jumble of events in our life.[31] So, for instance, I tell of my early
childhood as the introduction of an immigrant to a new land, my teenage
years as chapters about seeking achievement in school, the onset of
chronic back pain in college as a key turning point in following Jesus and
so on. In his *Confessions* Augustine himself edited and interpreted the
raw material of his life, shaping the final product into a meaningful story.
Narrative and narrative elements like main characters, plots, themes and
climaxes serve as the primary means by which we discern meaning in
life's happenings. Stories are such a primordial element of meaning that
entire communities depend on common tales, myths and histories for
shared identity and cohesion.[32]

Entire epochs are no different. Whether it is nineteenth-century America's story of Manifest Destiny or fourteenth-century Italy's tale of Renaissance, eras define themselves by some overarching narrative. Of course
epochs are actually formed by a very complex mix of social, economic,
religious, political and other forces. But an epoch nevertheless tends to
sum up all those forces in some coherent narrative. A narrative will hold
sway over an era to the extent that it offers some compelling, overarching
meaning.[33]

Often the epochal narrative accomplishes this by locating its own era
vis-à-vis other eras. For instance, the Renaissance defined itself by telling
a story of the previous epoch entitled the "Dark Ages." In this telling, the
Dark Ages had eclipsed an older, more glorious classical era, to which the
Renaissance was now returning.[34] Indeed, epochal stories have a strong
tendency to assume the pretensions of metanarrative. Thus the Enlightenment spun a tale of all previous eras as progressive struggles out of
superstition and irrationality so that it could tell the grand story of the tri-

---

[31]For an excellent discussion of how narrative is central to shaping one's identity, see
Charles Taylor, *Sources of the Self: The Making of the Modern Identity* (Cambridge, Mass.:
Harvard University Press, 1989), pp. 95-97.

[32]Stanley Hauerwas, *A Community of Character* (Notre Dame, Ind.: University of Notre
Dame Press, 1981).

[33]Middleton and Walsh, *Truth Is Stranger*, pp. 75-76.

[34]Norman Cantor has argued that the modern epoch "invented" the Middle Ages as part of
its own "epochal story." See his *Inventing the Middle Ages* (New York: William Morrow,
1991).

umph of science and reason—with its own era starring as the climax of that triumph.

An epochal challenge is a contest in storytelling. While an epochal challenge, like an epoch itself, is really made up of a web of complex forces, it too tends to sum up its challenge by presenting a rival story. It seeks to overturn and supplant the inherited story of the epoch with its own metanarrative. For example, postmodernism trumped the Enlightenment by interpreting all other epochal stories—especially the Enlightenment's—as stories of the naked "will to power" disguising itself under universal claims to truth.

The one who can tell the best story, in a very real sense, wins the epoch. History is replete with examples of epoch-defining power gained by superior storytelling. The Nazis came to power by "spinning" Germany's humiliating loss in World War I into a tale about a stab in the back by non-Aryan betrayers on the home front. This myth gained power as it incorporated Wagnerian legends of Teutonic glory, might and purity. The feebleness of the Weimar Republic was most evident in its complete failure to offer a compelling alternative story.[35] The recent era of tribal conflicts in places such as the former Yugoslavia and Northern Ireland was driven by the constant reawakening of old tales of injustice and bloodshed.[36] The apartheid era in South Africa relied on a complex set of Afrikaner religious and historical myths to justify the Nationalist regime.[37] On the positive side, mobilizing the American civil rights movement involved evoking a narrative of liberation that extended back to slavery, and even all the way back to the exodus story. Martin Luther King Jr. transformed American politics in the 1960s by connecting that story to the democratic narrative America told of itself. As his famous "I Have a Dream" speech declared, his dream was "deeply rooted in the American dream."[38]

Epochal stories need not necessarily take a historical form. The narra-

---

[35]Richard Bessel, *Germany After the First World War* (Oxford: Clarendon, 1993), pp. 254-84.

[36]Conor Cruise O'Brien, *Ancestral Voices: Religion and Nationalism in Ireland* (Chicago: University of Chicago Press, 1994), pp. 22-28.

[37]Allister Sparks, *The Mind of South Africa* (New York: Alfred A. Knopf, 1990), pp. 22-33.

[38]Taylor Branch, *Parting the Waters* (New York: Simon & Schuster, 1988), p. 882.

tives of epochs and their challengers can come in many different genres.
For instance, eras can be defined by certain scientific paradigms. Thomas
Kuhn, in his landmark study *The Structure of Scientific Revolutions*,
argued that scientific epochs are challenged and overturned in a contest
of paradigms.[39] Some scholars examining the history of science have
noted that particular paradigms like Darwinism or Freudian psychology
bear a strong narrative structure.[40] Economic theories that define a historical period, whether they be the laissez-faire mercantilism of eigh-
teenth-century England or the Keynesianism of the post-World War II
West, likewise rest on plot, genre, metaphors and other narrative elements.[41] Alasdair MacIntyre has argued persuasively that philosophers
and philosophical argument, for all their claim to operate in the realm of
pure abstraction, are ultimately intelligible only in the framework of specific traditions.[42] Strikingly, many of the classic philosophical arguments
from different traditions seem to take the form of a story: from Plato's
scene of the man bound to the chair in the cave to Hobbes's elaborate
drama of the "state of nature," to John Rawls's "choosing game."[43] Stories
may come in many different genres, but we cannot escape them.

### Can Stories Evaluate Each Other?

The inescapability of narrative in our efforts to grasp reality is a central
insight of postmodern thought. In my opinion this insight represents
postmodernism's most helpful contribution to Christian thinking. How-

---

[39]Thomas Kuhn, *The Structure of Scientific Revolutions* (Chicago: University of Chicago
Press, 1970).

[40]John Angus Campbell, "Charles Darwin: Rhetorician of Science," in *The Rhetoric of the
Human Sciences*, ed. John Nelson, Allan Megill and D. N. McCloskey (Madison: University
of Wisconsin Press, 1987), pp. 69-86; Kenneth Gergen and Mary M. Gergen, "Narrative
Form and the Construction of Psychological Science," in *Narrative Psychology: The Storied Nature of Human Conduct*, ed. T. R. Sarbin (New York: Praeger, 1986), pp. 22-44.

[41]Donald N. McCloskey, *If You're So Smart: The Narrative of Economic Expertise* (Chicago:
University of Chicago Press, 1990), pp. 25-55.

[42]Alasdair MacIntyre, *After Virtue* (Notre Dame, Ind.: University of Notre Dame Press,
1981).

[43]Plato *The Republic* 7, in *Dialogues of Plato*, trans. J. D. Kaplan (New York: Pocket, 1950),
pp. 357-63; Thomas Hobbes, *Leviathan*, in *Leviathan: Authoritative Text, Background and
Interpretations* (New York: W. W. Norton, 1997), pp. 68-79; John Rawls, *A Theory of Justice*
(Cambridge, Mass.: Harvard University Press, 1971), pp. 136-42.

ever, this contribution is not without its dangers. At the same time that postmodernism emphasizes story, it also strongly condemns the notion that any one story can capture another story. Any story's claim to meta-narrative status, according to the postmodern critic, only disguises how those in power suppress the marginalized. So, for example, the white Europeans' metanarrative of modernist rationality served only to keep Native Americans like Jake from claiming their own tribal stories and identity. Such oppressive uses of metanarrative led Jean-François Lyotard to "define 'postmodern' as incredulity toward meta-narratives."[44]

This incredulity extends to any attempt by one narrative to evaluate another. Since no story can claim ultimate truth, all stories are equally fictitious. For the most radical of postmoderns like Alex, they are "all made up in your head." You have your story, I have mine. My attempt to offer any correction of your story indeed ought to be shrugged off with a "So what?" In the postmodern encounter, each can at best only listen mutely to the other's tale.

Christian theologians who have embraced the postmodern emphasis of narrative frequently have shown a disturbing tendency to accept this condition of silence. Among narrative theologians there exists great reluctance to propose how one story can engage and even critically evaluate a different story. As a result, such theologians generally prefer not to speak about missions and evangelism, or do so only in very ambiguous terms.

Such reluctance and ambiguity are epitomized in the writing of theologian Stanley Hauerwas. Over the past couple of decades, perhaps no one has written more prolifically to call the church to embrace the post-modern emphasis on narrative. Hauerwas has argued persuasively that the church must be a "story formed" community: a group of people who embody the biblical narrative in their life together. Drawing heavily on the work of philosopher Alasdair MacIntyre, Hauerwas rejects any attempt to ground the church's proclamation in the modernist fiction of a universally acknowledged rationality. The church's witness is intelligi-

---

[44]Jean-François Lyotard, *The Postmodern Condition*, trans. Geoff Bennington and Brian Massumi (Minneapolis: University of Minnesota Press, 1984), p. xxiv.

ble only as the lived story of its community.[45]

But what then of the church's encounter with those outside its story and story-formed communal life? In his most influential book, *Community of Character*, Hauerwas declares, "The crucial interaction of story and community for the formation of truthful lives is an indication that there exists no 'story of stories' from which the many stories of our existence can be analyzed and evaluated."[46] He emphasizes repeatedly that "the task of Christians is not, therefore, to demonstrate that all other positions are false."[47] He acknowledges that this leads him to a "certain kind of relativism." However, he insists that his relativism is not necessarily total. He claims "there is no conceptual reason that prevents me from making judgments or from seeking to change the mind of those from other traditions" and that he even theoretically supports the sending of missionaries.[48] But Hauerwas never demonstrates exactly how he can have it both ways: holding on to his brand of relativism while still making evaluative judgments or supporting missions. To this reader, his philosophical position, which he calls a "non-vicious relativism," seems vague at best and incomprehensible at worst.

Not surprsingly, Hauerwas's conceptual vagueness translates into misiological vagueness. Practically speaking, how does a missionary of his nonvicious relativism school critically engage with another narrative tradition? On this question Hauerwas is mostly silent. The only advice he gives is postponement: only "after time" may such evaluative judgments "be appropriate."[49]

And in the meantime, what is an actual missionary supposed to say? Presumably Hauerwas would tell the missionary to develop a story-formed Christian community and then invite nonbelievers to witness the life of the community, for "witness derives from no other source than that which invites us to 'look what manner of life has been made

---

[45]Among the many books by Hauerwas that reiterate these themes are *Resident Aliens* (Nashville: Abingdon, 1989); *Theology Without Foundations* (Nashville: Abingdon, 1994); and *Christian Existence Today* (Durham, N.C.: Labyrinth, 1988).

[46]Hauerwas, *Community of Character*, p. 96.

[47]Ibid., p. 94.

[48]Ibid., pp. 101, 105.

[49]Ibid., p. 105.

possible among us by the power of the cross and resurrection of Christ.' " But what would the missionary preach to unbelievers so that this community could come into being in the first place? And even once it came into being, how would she or he preach so that a non-believer dwelling in a different story and community would actually bother to examine—much less switch into—the Christian story and community? Hauerwas offers no answer, other than repeating that the evangelistic process is decidedly *not* based "on the assumption that there is something wrong with the others' beliefs."[50] For Hauerwas, evangelism ends up as an only vaguely endorsed and rather unexplainable phenomenon.

Of course no human can offer an ultimate explanation for successful missions and conversions; the church's existence and any individual's conversion are profoundly mysterious acts of God. But seeking ultimate explanations for such mysteries is not the same as helping evangelists and missionaries to engage critically with rival stories. The former is reserved solely for God's majestic revelation at the end of time; the latter has been the sweaty labor of the church's teachers and thinkers in every epoch. To put this another way, suppose Marcellinus and Ramon of Penyaforte had mailed their questions to Stanley Hauerwas. I may be simplifying, but based on his writing it appears that Hauerwas could only write back: "Postpone dealing with such questions, and just point to your own Christian community." Those missionaries would have read such a correspondence with disappointment. They needed something more.

And so do we. It seems to me that Hauerwas epitomizes both the promise and danger of postmodernity for Christian thought. Certainly any word addressed to the non-Christian—and especially to the postmodern challenger—must be accompanied by lives embodying the message. Hauerwas's insistence on the narrative nature of truth and his loud calls for Christian communities to live out the radical nature of the gospel story ring as prophetic words. But Hauerwas also exemplifies the weakness of such a postmodern perspective when left unaccompanied by any

---

[50]Ibid.

clear strategy for how one story can critically engage another.[51] That such
a vigorous voice as Hauerwas's can offer only a feeble picture of rhetorical engagement highlights the need for a robust internarrative strategy.
We need answers to the question: How can today's Christian storyteller
critically engage postmodern storytellers face to face?

As I have already said, I believe reestablishing a correspondence with
Augustine and Aquinas can help us address this question. Their shared
strategy of "taking every thought captive" involves deliberately measuring
the challenger's story for engagement. They exhibit confidence that their
"story of stories" can equip missionaries and evangelists to speak. Whether
their confidence was warranted in their day and whether their underlying
strategy empowers us today are questions that occupy the pages to come.

### Literature Surrounding *City of God* and *Summa contra Gentiles*

Arguing my thesis will necessarily involve a comparative reading of *City
of God* and *Summa contra Gentiles*. In the process I hope to offer some
additional contributions to the study of these two texts. The scholarly
treatment of these works, as far as I can tell, is marked by an almost total
absence of comparative analysis with each other.[52] This is not surprising
given the increasing specialization in disciplines like church history, but
it is unfortunate given that *City of God* and *Summa contra Gentiles* so
defined their respective eras. If for no other reason than a purely historical one, their comparison is long overdue.

Where Augustine's and Aquinas's general bodies of thought are compared, the comparison usually focuses on some restricted question, such as
their views on various political arrangements, the role of women or the use of
logic.[53] I hope to show that their underlying strategy of response to epochal

---

[51]For further reflections on the problem of how a narrative emphasis makes difficult any
critical leverage over rival stories, see George Lindbeck, *The Nature of Doctrine: Religion
and Theology in a Post-liberal Age* (Philadelphia: Westminster Press, 1984).

[52]A search of Harvard University's library system (HOLLIS) contained no entries fitting this
description.

[53]For example, see Ernest L. Fortin, *Classical Christianity and the Political Order* (Lanham,
Md.: Rowman & Littlefield, 1996); Kari Elisabeth Borresen, *Subordination and Equiva-
lence: The Nature and Role of Women in Augustine and Thomas Aquinas* (Washington,
D.C.: University Press of America, 1981); Robert H. Ayers, *Language, Logic and Reason in*

challenges reveals a more comprehensive unity between these two thinkers.

Such a focus also reveals a deeper unity *within* each individual text. *City of God* and *Summa contra Gentiles* are massive works, sprawling over numerous subtopics and following many complex paths of inquiry. Academic study of these works has produced no clear consensus on how to map out their overall structure. Scholars still struggle to discern a framework that unites all the disparate sections. John O'Meara opens his introduction of the most widely used edition of *City of God* with the observation: "Few books have given rise to so much misconception as the *City of God*. By some it is thought to give a philosophy, by others a theology of history. By some it is thought to contain well developed political theories."[54] Later on O'Meara himself shrugs his shoulders and concludes that many books in *City of God* cannot be viewed in a broader unity.[55] Thomas Merton introduced another popular edition of *City of God* by going so far as to claim that Augustine must have changed his intention in writing the book midway in the text, leaving the book in two disjointed halves.[56]

Similarly, the question of the overall intention that unites *Summa contra Gentiles* has been the subject of much academic debate. I have included an appendix on this debate, since my reading will especially conflict with the works of some recent and influential scholars. The issue is critical, for it involves the very coherence of Aquinas's thought. Thomist scholar Anton Pegis, who translated the most widely used edition of *Summa contra Gentiles*, summarized the stakes involved:

> This work is one of the great expressions of the thought of St. Thomas Aquinas. It is, in many ways, the most personal of his doctrinal writings. Strangely enough, however, the SCG finds no unanimity of opinion among

---

the Church Fathers: A Study of Tertullian, Augustine and Aquinas (New York: Olms, 1979). Of course there are several works like Norman Cantor's *Medieval Thought: Augustine and Thomas Aquinas* (Waltham, Mass.: Blaisdell, 1969) that present general introductions to both of these thinkers. Most of these, like Cantor's book, do not attempt any comparative analysis of the two in general, much less specifically of *City of God* and *Summa contra Gentiles*.

[54]O'Meara, introduction to *COG*, p. vii.

[55]Ibid., p. xxxvi.

[56]Thomas Merton, introduction to *City of God* (New York: Modern Library, 1950), p. x.

the historians and students of St. Thomas. There is disagreement as to the nature and purpose of the work. There is disagreement as to its general organization and the articulation of its doctrine. . . . These disagreements *bear on nothing less than the interpretation of the Thomism of St. Thomas himself in its most fundamental aspects.* In the presence of the SCG, the issue is not one of maintaining a coherent interpretation of particular texts on a particular problem, *but of seeing the SCG in the unity that inspired it.*[57]

Like *City of God, Summa contra Gentiles* begs for a reading that will restore it to a unified whole.

So while I unapologetically pursue the practical agenda of engaging postmodern unbelief, I also seek to engage the academic community with a vision of the coherent purpose and unity of both these seminal works. For both *Summa contra Gentiles* and *City of God,* I hope to show that keeping in mind the strategy of "taking every thought captive" will explain their overall organization, as well as various maneuvers these authors make that otherwise might seem disjointed.

In short, I hope to reopen some important lines of communication: between Augustine and Aquinas, between various sections within each individual work and finally between these great thinkers and us. The particular strategy of "taking every thought captive" serves as the topic for all these correspondences.

### A Postscript: The Work of Alasdair MacIntyre

The work of Alasdair MacIntyre casts a long shadow—or more aptly, a bright light—over all Christian thinkers seeking to engage with postmodernism. In a trilogy of brilliant, groundbreaking books, *After Virtue* (1984), *Whose Justice? Which Rationality?* (1988) and *Three Rival Versions of Moral Enquiry* (1990), this Catholic philosopher has illuminated many of the issues addressed in this book, especially how different traditions can or cannot engage with one another. Among the many debts I owe to his work is his repeated effort to connect Aquinas to these pressing questions. Readers who are unfamiliar with his work may simply note my gratitude and spare themselves this somewhat technical postscript. However, for

---

[57]Pegis, introduction to *SCG* 1, p. 20, emphasis mine.

those who have more closely followed MacIntyre, it may be helpful to
note how I differ from his program generally and his appropriation of
Aquinas specifically.

Most simply stated, I believe that MacIntyre's penetrating analysis of
our situation is largely correct, but I am dubious of his programmatic pro-
posal. MacIntyre believes the way out of our postmodern impasse lies in a
premodern tradition of discourse. He advocates the tradition known as
Thomism, a highly structured form of dialectical debate that uses Aristotelian categories and has been especially utilized within the Roman Catholic Church.

In *After Virtue*, the first of his trilogy, MacIntyre most clearly argues for
the superiority of the premodern Aristotelian tradition as a response to
the philosophical challenges confronting us today. However, he admits at
the end of that book that Aristotelianism is not a Christian tradition per
se and thus he still needs to examine the "reconciliation of biblical theology and Aristotelianism."[58] In the second and third books, MacIntyre
seeks to show how Thomas Aquinas achieved this reconciliation and thus
served as a key link in the ongoing development of this ancient tradition.
In subsequent centuries of dialectical debate, Aquinas's followers
extended this premodern tradition to us today in the form of Thomism.
The ancient (going back to Aristotle and the Greeks) and continuous
(achieved by Aquinas and followers) qualities of this tradition are what
define Thomism as a superior mode of discourse.[59] Only Thomism can
provide an empowering lineage to guide us in our rootless epoch.

Despite MacIntyre's complex and considerable philosophical accomplishments, I question whether his preferred tradition can ultimately
underwrite an effective rhetorical strategy for this epoch. Pragmatically, I
have little hope that evangelists, apologists and preachers imbued with
Aristotelian/Thomistic categories can adequately speak to a postmodern
audience. Returning to a distinctively premodern tradition of discourse,
with its highly dialectical structure of argument and ancient philosophical

---

[58]MacIntyre, *After Virtue*, p. 278.
[59]MacIntyre, *Three Rival Versions*, p. 77. In this work MacIntyre also argues that Aquinas
was essentially trying to reconcile the inherited Augustinianism with the new Aristotelianism.

terminology, simply will not help us engage people like Jake and Alex.

Yet I do not believe that leaving behind Thomism the tradition means jettisoning Aquinas the author. There is a distinction, and it can be found in MacIntyre's own work. One of the peculiar traits of MacIntyre's trilogy is that for all its advocacy of Thomism, it includes very little extended textual analysis of Aquinas's own words. In the only chapters that come close to an attempt (chapters ten to twelve in *Whose Justice? Which Rationality?*), he draws from an eclectic sampling and only makes one passing reference to *Summa contra Gentiles*.[60] This is especially ironic given that MacIntyre's account of Aquinas is so highly influential in contemporary moral and political theory.

I hope to appropriate Aquinas differently—by paying close attention to his own words in his "most personal" work. The attentive reader of Aquinas can properly claim inheritance to a rhetorical strategy other than Thomism. This strategy is better characterized as a drama rather than a tradition, as creative tellings of the gospel story rather than dialectical arguments extended over time. Furthermore, if my comparative reading of *City of God* and *Summa contra Gentiles* is correct, this strategy can also claim an illustrious lineage going back to the first centuries of the church. Most important, I hope that this inheritance can guide new, creative and distinctively postmodern ways of Christian proclamation.

### What Follows

To summarize, Christians today face an epochal challenge. Like all epochal challenges, postmodernism threatens the church's existing paradigms and harmony with the broader society. As the old understandings break down and new conflicts break out, Christians especially need a new rhetorical strategy. In the postmodern epoch a satisfactory strategy must take into account the narrative nature of meaning in general and of epochal challenges in particular. While being sensitive to narrative, however, such a strategy must retain an ability to critically engage with rival stories if it is to be of any use to the church's teachers, missionaries and

---

[60]Alasdair MacIntyre, *Whose Justice? Which Rationality?* (Notre Dame, Ind.: University of Notre Dame Press, 1988), p. 192.

evangelists. Such a strategy, which I call "taking every thought captive," can be found in a long-overdue comparison between *City of God* and *Summa contra Gentiles*. Hopefully, the strategy will also provide a much-needed unifying reading of each of these classic texts.

What follows further develops the themes introduced in this chapter. Chapter two undertakes a historical comparison of Augustine and Aquinas. For each period, I seek to lay out the previously dominant epochal story and the new challengers' rival story. This chapter also seeks to depict how the personal life stories of these authors helped shape their unique responses. Chapters three and four are extended readings of *City of God* and *Summa contra Gentiles,* respectively. As such, they represent the core of my argument. Chapter five concludes by assessing the legacy of these two texts and suggesting possible implications for our response to the postmodern challenge of today.

# 2

# Augustine & Aquinas
## A HISTORICAL COMPARISON

A CHRISTIAN CONTEMPORARY OF AUGUSTINE would have approached the end of the fourth century believing his epoch was a special one. His epoch was distinguished by its stark contrast to the previous one, which might have been titled the "Age of Martyrs." Tales of earlier Christians dying at the hands of imperial persecutors were well preserved by his generation. In such tales the evil villain would have been played by past pagan emperors like Decius, who in 250 ordered the first major government campaign against the church, or Diocletian, who in 303 led the last major persecution. The average Christian church of that time celebrated an elaborate liturgical cycle to recount the story of a small minority persevering within a hostile society.[1]

### Augustine's Inherited Epoch
Yet the story of the past epoch could be so freely celebrated only because conditions were so different now. In popular retellings, the turning point had arrived with great dramatic flair. Close to ninety years earlier, before a key battle to determine who would rule the Roman Empire, Constan-

---

[1]Robert Markus, *The End of Ancient Christianity* (Cambridge: Cambridge University Press, 1990), pp. 97-106.

tine had seen a divine vision promising him victory and had converted to Christianity. He went into battle bearing the Greek monogram of the first letters of Christ's name on his standards, and his ensuing victory and ascendancy to power introduced a new era. He decreed a general policy of toleration for Christianity and persuaded his eastern colleague, the pagan Licinius, to do so as well. He made it legally possible for the church to own property for the first time. And he would wield imperial power to enforce consensus within the church at the historic Council of Nicaea and in other controversies.[2]

As a result, in a few short decades Christianity went from being a persecuted minority cult to a growing religion that enjoyed favored status. The "Constantinian revolution" triggered such an explosive spread of Christianity that the towns and central provinces of the Empire became dominated by Christians. Even nonbelievers acknowledged that the era seemed to be a "Christian" one.[3] Although Augustine presented a unique conception of the era, he too used the term "Christian era" as a widely accepted shorthand for this historical period.[4]

The dramatic spread of Christianity had many complex causes, but the church's union with Rome certainly contributed heavily. With state support, "the Church's wealth, prestige, and power grew, as did its influence in public affairs. . . . Social pressures toward conformity played a far greater part in sweeping the masses into the Christian Church."[5] Advancing in the imperial civil service often necessitated becoming a Christian.[6] The progress of the era seemed to move ever closer to a complete union between church and state. In 382 the emperor Gratian disendowed the Roman pagan cults, which had depended on government subsidy and sanction. Contemporaries viewed this move (prematurely, as we shall see) as the formal "end of

---

[2]Ramsay MacMullen, *Christianizing the Roman Empire* (New Haven, Conn.: Yale University Press, 1984), pp. 43-51.

[3]Robert Markus, *Saeculum* (London: Cambridge University Press, 1970), pp. 35-36.

[4]See, for example, *COG* 4.1, pp. 134-35.

[5]Robert Markus, *Christianity in the Roman World* (London: Thames and Hudson, 1974), p. 123.

[6]Ibid., p. 90.

paganism in Rome."[7] The withdrawal of official support of other religions quickly advanced to outright persecution. In 399 Augustine himself saw imperial agents arriving in Africa to close pagan shrines.[8] This cultural about-face culminated at the turn of the century with Emperor Theodosius, in a recapitulation of the Constantinian motif, defeating his pagan rival Flavianus in battle and subsequently declaring Christianity the official religion of the Empire. The Theodosian establishment appeared to mark the final stage in the construction of one regime, fully Roman and fully Christian.[9]

### The Epochal Story: The Eternal City

The story summarizing this epoch for the church might aptly be titled "The Eternal City." Constantine and subsequent Christian emperors like Theodosius were, according to this story, the fulfillment of a divine plan ordained before time to join the church and Rome as one entity. Eusebius served as the master storyteller of this metanarrative. Eusebius summed up in his own person the story of union: he was both a church historian (the very first one, by most accounts) and the official biographer of Constantine. Robert Markus describes the narrative structure of Eusebius's most famous work, *Ecclesiastical History*:

> Verses which had traditionally been interpreted in the Church in a messianic sense, are now boldly referred to the person of Constantine. . . . The final recension of this last book of his great work is written quite uninhibitedly to celebrate the first Christian emperor as the culmination of God's marvelous saving work. Constantine brings to a fulfillment what God himself had prepared in Christ and Augustus: he brings about the unification of the world in a single harmonious order, one Empire devoted to the worship of the one true God.[10]

---

[7]Peter Brown, *Religion and Society in the Age of St. Augustine* (New York: Harper & Row, 1972), pp. 163-64; see pp. 161-83 for a detailed discussion of the variety of factors behind the Christianization of the Roman aristocracy.

[8]Peter Brown, *Augustine of Hippo* (Berkeley: University of California Press, 1969), p. 231.

[9]Markus, *Saeculum*, pp. 28, and Peter Brown, *The World of Late Antiquity* (London: Thames and Hudson, 1971), p. 106.

[10]Markus, *Saeculum*, pp. 49-50.

The eternal aspect of Eusebius's story was especially emphasized: the church-Rome marriage formed one "single harmonious order" that was destined to last forever as the "culmination of God's marvelous saving work."

"The Eternal City" was embraced by both sides of the aisle. Constantine called the bishops his "dearest brothers" and vowed to be forever joined to the church. In fact, the emperor claimed "he was the thirteenth Apostle, to be buried alongside the memorials of the Twelve, and housed in the new church of the Holy Apostles being built next to his new palace in his new capital."[11] The church similarly reassembled the imperial scenery for itself. Church architecture in this period took on Roman imperial forms, while church art was dominated by iconography that depicted Christ as an emperor.[12] A Christian bishop assumed that Christianity and Roman civilization would be so linked through all times that he could not even imagine a non-Roman Christian. He ridiculed the prospect that "Christian virtue could exist among the barbarians!"[13]

As an epochal story the "Eternal City" assumed the historical genre. It gathered the chronology of Rome and Christianity and imposed an overarching narrative that explained various specific events. Melito of Sardis ascribed "the flourishing of the Roman Empire since its foundation by Augustus to the excellence of the Christian religion established during his reign."[14] As a metanarrative the "Eternal City" claimed that Rome's marriage with Christianity was not merely a historical event but actually the consummation of history itself. Reading Eusebius's *Ecclesiastical History*, Christians were easily "lured into believing that a new messianic age had dawned with Constantine's conversion."[15] All historical events could be interpreted through the story's eschatological nature. Thus the Dalmatian bishop Hesychius would write to Augustine exuberantly celebrating the geographical spread of Christianity to the boundaries of the Roman Empire; surely this meant that "the Gospel has been

---

[11]Markus, *Christianity in the Roman World*, pp. 100-101.
[12]Ibid., pp. 101-3.
[13]Quoted in Brown, *Augustine of Hippo*, p. 26.
[14]Markus, *Christianity in the Roman World*, p. 29
[15]Markus, *End of Ancient Christianity*, p. 89.

preached to the ends of the earth"—the biblical prerequisite for the end times.[16] Augustine, as we shall see, was uniquely positioned to puncture Hesychius's buoyant assertion. But to almost everyone else the current historical era represented the final chapter, a chapter that would go on into eternity.

It should be noted that Rome, the actual physical city, still took center stage in this narrative. Rome had long proclaimed itself in its own myths as the *civitas aeternitas*. Now it was united with the kingdom of God to constitute a truly eternal society. Even though Constantine had founded another capital in the East in 330 and the imperial court had moved to Ravenna by the fifth century, the city of Rome was still widely acknowledged as the center of Roman civilization. Even pagans still venerated Rome as the holy city. The church actively shared in this staging. Late-fourth-century popes would seek to foster the centrality of Rome, especially by cultivating the legends of Peter's and Paul's burials on the Vatican Hill.[17]

### The Epochal Challenge: The Pagans' Counterhistory

The marriage of Christianity with Rome did not go uncontested. Even in this Christian era, paganism retained a deep hold on Roman culture. The spread of Christianity predictably provoked a hostile response. Julian the Apostate's brief campaign of persecution was the most obvious example of pagan attempts to violently exterminate the "novel religion."[18] Augustine was well aware of this threat. At the very beginning of the fifth century, pagan mobs in North Africa reacted to the destruction of the local cult statue of Hercules by killing sixty Christians.[19]

Recent scholarship has documented that Christians perpetrated their share of violence in the conflict. For instance, at around the same time Augustine began writing *City of God*, news spread from Alexandria that a Christian mob had lynched and burned a prominent female anti-Chris-

---

[16]Markus, *Saeculum*, p. 39.

[17]Brown, *World of Late Antiquity*, pp. 121-22.

[18]Peter Brown, *Society and the Holy in Late Antiquity* (Berkeley: University of California Press, 1982), pp. 83-102.

[19]Markus, *Christianity in the Roman World*, p. 127.

tian orator named Hypatia. Augustine himself had to warn his congregation against taking the law into their own hands and assaulting pagan property.[20]

Although the pagan challenge involved physical violence, the conflict was most consistently fought in the intellectual realm. The challenge was spearheaded by a cadre of upper-class, educated elites. Volusianus, the pagan proconsul who was the subject of Marcellinus's request to Augustine, was a notable representative of this group and its orientation. They were archconservatives who were "anxious to invest their beliefs in a distant, golden past, untroubled by the rise of Christianity."[21] Markus sums up their worldview:

> Theirs was no mere learned antiquarianism. It was a devotion to the Roman past in which their aristocratic tastes, their pagan religion and their classical culture fused in a single-minded attachment to a tradition under threat of extinction. The rising Christian tide was threatening to engulf their world; with quiet passion and subdued tenacity these last Romans of Rome were trying to keep alive a whole way of life and feeling, of thought, imagination and public ritual.[22]

These pagan intellectuals channeled their "quiet passion and subdued tenacity" toward shaping the worldview of the day in opposition to Christianity. Augustine was well aware of how even in his congregations the pagan worldview could assert itself either as an outright rival or as a subtle corrupter of belief.[23] Pagans monopolized the institutions of learning in much the same way the "cultured despisers of Christianity" do today.[24] As intellectuals do in almost any era, these pagan elites sought to define how their era interpreted events.

The seminal event that would demand interpretation came in 410 with Alaric's sack of Rome. In retrospect, scholars have listed many complex

---

[20]Ramsay MacMullen, *Christianity and Paganism in the Fourth to Eighth Centuries* (New Haven, Conn.: Yale University Press, 1997), pp. 14-15.

[21]Brown, *Augustine of Hippo*, p. 301.

[22]Markus, *Christianity in the Roman World*, p. 130-31.

[23]Brown, *Augustine of Hippo*, p. 269.

[24]The term is, of course, Friedrich Schleiermacher's. See George Marsden, *The Soul of the University: From Protestant Establishment to Established Nonbelief* (New York: Oxford University Press, 1994).

reasons for the fall of Rome. Political, cultural and socioeconomic divisions were fragmenting Roman society. It was not strong enough to keep outsiders like the barbarians at bay, nor flexible enough to absorb them as immigrants.[25] The previous century had witnessed numerous collapses along the frontiers of the Empire. Only military reforms, higher taxes and other reforms of Constantine had in 324 staved off the barbarian threat, and even then only temporarily. By 378 Visigoths had defeated the Eastern division of the Roman army at Adrianople. In 402 they crossed the Danube frontier and penetrated Italy proper.

Nevertheless, to contemporaries the collapse of Rome in 410 came as an utter shock. The average Roman believed that although various frontiers might fall, the Western soldier and civilization would continue to dominate the barbarian world as they had for centuries.[26] This confidence was shared and reinforced by all Christians. Rome was God's holy city in their story; surely God would cause it to endure and prosper through history!

The events of 410 thus provided pagan challengers with a perfect opportunity to deconstruct the story of the Eternal City and replace it with their own. The epochal challenge likewise was presented in the historical genre. The historical genre naturally suited these pagans who so looked to the past as their ideal and authority. They focused their counterhistory on the events leading up to the fall of Rome.

Their story included three subplots: a history of Rome's politics, a history of Rome's religion, and a history of Rome's philosophy. Each of these interrelated subplots was narrated to depict the union of Christianity and Rome as a novel corruption of Rome's ideal past, a corruption that explained the recent decay.

### The Three Subplots of the Challengers' Story

The pagans' political history centered on Rome's destiny. As Manifest Destiny did for America or the Thousand-Year Third Reich did for Germany, Rome's promised future as Empire defined Rome's politics. This

---

[25]Brown, *World of Late Antiquity*, p. 122.
[26]Ibid., pp. 22-27, 112, 118.

political destiny was rooted in ancient history, as told by Virgil's *Aeneid* and other classical legends.[27] Such legends rooted Rome's glorious destiny in events that occurred long before Constantine and along a narrative stream radically divergent from Eusebius's *Ecclesiastical History.* The need to remain true to the ancient political foundations of the city had consistently justified pagan challenges to Christianity. In 311 Emperor Galerius explained past persecutions of Christians by claiming, "We wished previously, always acting for the good of the commonwealth, to correct all things according to the ancient laws and public discipline of the Romans."[28]

In the pagan explanation, then, the sack of Rome was a conclusive demonstration of what happened to the society when it sought a new political destiny and abandoned its past. The Christian destiny of the Eternal City story was shown to be foreign and ultimately untrustworthy. Augustine refers to this rival interpretation in the opening pages of *City of God*: "[Pagans] now complain of this Christian era, and hold Christ responsible for the disasters which their city endured. . . . They attribute their deliverance [from further destruction] to *their own destiny.*"[29]

This political subplot was closely linked to a religious history. The pagans also emphasized rigorous maintenance of the city's ancient religious rites. Roman paganism was never a set of abstract principles or universal truths; it was all about local communities carefully preserving local cultic practices.[30] Each city had its own divine patron appeased by rituals that had developed over centuries. The older the ritual, the more esteemed was the practice. Indeed, pagan conservatives would express bafflement as to why Christians would replace a venerable religious tradition handed down by their Jewish ancestors with radically new ritu‧ als.[31]

The importance of maintaining ancient rituals stirred great passion

[27]Markus, *Christianity in the Roman World,* p. 130.
[28]Quoted in ibid., p. 86.
[29]*COG* 1.1, p. 6, emphasis mine.
[30]Brown, *World of Late Antiquity,* p. 60.
[31]Brown, *Augustine of Hippo,* p. 316. It was, in fact, the tinge of antiquity in Judaism that had always made Judaism acceptable to the Roman world.

among the pagans. It was no accident that in the period preceding the sack of Rome, the pagan elite rallied their forces most urgently to combat Emperor Gratian's decision to disendow the pagan altars at the center of the city. Symmachus, a pagan senator leading this challenge, especially fought to reinstate the Altar of Victory in the Senate Hall.[32] Christians, led by Bishop Ambrose, soundly defeated him by reminding the emperor of his obligations as a Christian. Ambrose would celebrate his victory over Symmachus as another glorious chapter in the story of the Eternal City.[33]

But after 410 the pagans would have material to rewrite that event as *the* criminal act in Rome's religious history. The capture of Rome simply represented the verdict of its neglected gods. Augustine notes this religious subplot of the epochal challenge in book one of *City of God:* "Why do our antagonists bring false accusations against the established Christian order, alleging that catastrophe has come upon the city just because it has left off the worship of its gods?"[34]

The pagan strategy of defeating the "established Christian order" by resorting to the past extended to its history of philosophy. Pagans traced their philosophy as far back as they could, back even beyond Rome to the ancient Greeks. They especially sought to establish continuity with that paragon of Hellenistic philosophy, Plato. Peter Brown summarizes the pagan Neo-Platonists:

> They competed with the Christians. . . . The great Platonists of their age, Plotinus and Porphyry, could provide them with a profoundly religious view of the world, that grew naturally out of an immemorial tradition. The claims of the Christian, by contrast, lacked intellectual foundation.[35]

As the philosophy with an older history, Neo-Platonism, in their view, possessed greater authority than Christianity.

This historical authority of Plato could be wielded against the "eternal" in the Eternal City story. The Platonic worldview sneered at

---

[32]Markus, *Christianity in the Roman World*, p. 125.
[33]Brown, *Augustine of Hippo*, pp. 70-71.
[34]*COG* 1.15, p. 25.
[35]Brown, *Augustine of Hippo*, p. 301

change; the immutable was the ideal. Plato's *Republic*, that paradigm of a stable civilization, thus stood in implicit judgment against all the roiling changes Christianity had introduced to Rome. More important, Neo-Platonists like Plotinus interpreted the tradition to mean that humans could, by their own reason and contemplation, lift the soul up to the truly immutable realm of the Eternal Ideal. This directly challenged the very climax of the Eternal City story: Christ joining Roman civilization to lead humankind to salvation with God. Augustine highlighted this aspect of their challenge:

> There are some men who consider themselves able to refine themselves on their own, in order to contemplate and remain in God. . . . They can promise themselves such refinement through their own efforts, because a few of them really were able to carry their minds beyond all created things and touch, however partially, the light of unchanging truth. Accordingly, they look down upon the mass of Christians who live on faith alone, as not being yet able to do as they do.[36]

In summary, the pagans fashioned the political, religious and philosophical subplots of Rome into an interpretation of history that challenged the Eternal City narrative. Any response to this epochal challenge needed to respond to each of those subplots.

### Augustine: Bilingual and On the Margins

Augustine's distinctive response to this epochal clash did not spring up ex nihilo. In two remarkable aspects, his personal history prepared him to respond to the epochal challenge. First, Augustine received excellent "bilingual" training: his own life story would immerse him in the pagan learning as well as in that of "the Eternal City." Second, Augustine would spend significant time on the margins of his inherited epoch. As a result, he was never inextricably bound to the inherited story of the Eternal City.

Nothing illustrates the bilingual nature of Augustine's early development better than his journey to the vicinity of Rome as a young man. He arrived only months after the battle between Bishop Ambrose and Sym-

---

[36]Quoted in ibid., pp. 103-4.

machus had reached its climax in the Altar of Victory controversy.[37] At
the time Augustine was not yet a believer. He had just completed a classical education of which any pagan would have enthusiastically
approved. He was hoping for a position as a professor of rhetoric, a post
that required him to deliver addresses on the glories of Rome's past in
careful emulation of Virgil and other classic historians. He had jour-
neyed to Rome to seek sponsors for his job search. The influential
patron he found was Symmachus. Symmachus secured him a post as
professor in Milan, seeking to add another protégé to his cadre of pagan
intellectuals.[38]

A few short years later Augustine sat in church as a new convert, listening intently to none other than Ambrose. (We can only wonder what
Augustine did if he ever ran into Symmachus on the street as he came out
of Ambrose's church!) Ambrose would significantly influence Augustine's
early intellectual development as a Christian. Milan was a seasonal resi-
dence of the imperial court and a center of the church-and-Rome union.
Augustine undoubtedly watched the politically powerful bishop dominate
the public life of Milan, daily enacting the story of the Eternal City. Later
Augustine spent time in the city of Rome itself.[39]

Yet for all his exposure to the centers of the epoch, Augustine spent
the bulk of his life on its margins. He was born in North Africa, and there
he served as bishop and wrote all his most important works. Through the
last thirty-five years of his life, this remote province shaped his worldview
in highly distinctive ways. Living at the periphery of the Empire, he
would realize that there were plenty of peoples whom the story of the
Eternal City had marginalized. From that vantage point, for example, he
would in *City of God* interpret the biblical prophecy that "the tents of
the Ethiopians will cower in fear, also the pavilions of the land of Mid-
ian" to mean "that is, the nations, suddenly terrified at the news of your
[God's] wonderful deeds, will form part of the Christian people, even

---

[37]O'Meara, introduction to *COG*, p. xi.

[38]On Augustine's education, see Brown, *Augustine of Hippo*, pp. 35-39; on his relationship
to Symmachus, see pp. 69-70.

[39]On Augustine's relationship to Ambrose, see Brown, *Augustine of Hippo*, pp. 35-39. For his
travels during this period, see pp. 73-75.

those nations who are not under Roman rule."[40] To Bishop Hesychius's buoyant assertion that the gospel had already gone forth to all the nations, Augustine would reply wryly, "There are among us, *that is in Africa,* innumerable barbarian tribes among whom the gospel has not yet been preached . . . yet it cannot rightly be said that the promise of God does not concern them."[41] This was a concept, as mentioned above, that most Christian bishops living at the center of the Eternal City dismissed as ludicrous.

The African church included thinkers who were more dubious of the church's union with Rome than Eusebius was. In Tertullian and Cyprian the church had a history of prickly wariness of Rome's central authority.[42] While Augustine would use imperial force to repress the Donatist heretics, he did so reluctantly. In the aftermath of the Donatist conflict Augustine would wrestle with serious apprehensions about the effectiveness of state coercion. His thinking in this matter was very complex, shifting and controversial. While scholars debate how much he actually changed his views in later life, it is important to note that his justification for imperial coercion of the Donatists rested on the fact that these were heretics of the Christian faith, not barbarian unbelievers. He makes a crucial distinction between relying on Christian rulers to correct those who had once been genuine Christians (and still called themselves such) and evangelizing nonbelievers.[43]

Moreover, it is quite likely that Augustine was influenced by a Donatist theologian's scathing critique of the Catholic Church's marriage to Rome.[44] The African Catholic Church itself stood as a bulwark against the "all roads lead to Rome" ecclesiology of the Eternal City story. The churches of this region organized the series of great African councils that implicitly questioned if not explicitly contested the bishop of Rome's

---

[40]*COG* 18.32, p. 801.

[41]Augustine, *Letters,* trans. W. Parsons (New York: Fathers of the Church, 1955), pp. 393-96, emphasis mine.

[42]James J. O'Donnell, *Augustine* (Boston: Twayne, 1985), pp. 1-2.

[43]Brown, Augustine of Hippo, pp. 233-43, 412.

[44]This was Tyconius, a Donatist theologian in North Africa. See Markus, *Saeculum,* p. 118

absolute dominance.[45] This feisty African spirit undoubtedly nurtured a
healthy independence in Augustine's thought: he would respond to the
epochal challenge, but not out of slavish allegiance to the inherited epoch.

### Thomas Aquinas's Inherited Epoch

The centuries following Augustine (d. 430) reflected a curious resolution
of the epochal challenge he faced. A few decades after his death, the
Roman Empire collapsed, weakened by further barbarian invasions and
fiscal crisis.[46] Without the Empire, the pagan elite class itself dissolved,
consigned to the past it so revered. The Empire's collapse also left a serious vacuum of any secular social institutions to unite diverse local communities. Western society as a whole faced dissolution, teetering on the
edge of total fragmentation. Christianity stepped into the void left by the
Empire and took over as the unifying force of the entire civilization. It
was as if with the death of her imperial husband, the widowed church
now assumed control over the entire household, stripped the Empire and
all others from the deed, and made it completely her own.

Pope Leo I literally attempted this with postimperial Rome. Peter
Brown documents Leo's "programme of turning Rome into a new and
radically Christian civic community . . . establishing the city as a *theop-
olis;* and his exercise of episcopal authority in what should have been
matters of secular justice has been seen as a step on the road towards
papal domination of the City." In this assumption of all social functions,
"Rome and its bishop may have been ahead of other Western towns, but
not unique."[47] In most towns the average citizen would now look to the
bishop to organize local defense, repair town walls, educate children,
make loans, provide public entertainment and address any other important social issue.[48] Even with the rise of the Carolingian state, the idea of

---

[45]For an excellent discussion of the North African ecclesiological tradition, see ibid., pp.
     105-32.
[46]While most historians agree that the end of the Western empire cannot be pinned to a spe-
     cific date, most mark A.D. 476, with the end of the reign of Romulus Augustus, as the sym
     bolic date of its demise. See Brown, *World of Late Antiquity,* pp. 126-28.
[47]Ibid., p. 127.
[48]Richard Fletcher, *The Barbarian Conversion* (New York: Henry Holt, 1997), pp. 50-51. See
     also Markus, *Christianity in the Roman World,* p. 144.

a purely secular power was meaningless. Brown sums up the scholarly consensus surrounding what happened during the first few centuries after the complete collapse of the Roman Empire: "Nobody seriously doubts that in ways such as these Western Europe was being drained of the 'secular' in these centuries."[49]

With no rival "secular" force around, Western Christianity increasingly conceived of itself as the universal society. The importance of this self-conception can be measured by the lengths to which the early medieval church went to repress sects that threatened its universalism in any way. The Dominican order, which Aquinas was to join, was founded to combat the Albigensians or Cathari heretics who separated themselves from the Catholic world. The first four Lateran councils similarly sought to establish a uniformity of belief. Michael Novak argues that such extreme measures were taken because the church viewed heresy as a threat to the very social order: "The chief consensual bond among people was Catholic faith and Catholic ritual. Virtually all unifying conceptions of relationship and social weight, meaning and order, came from that faith."[50] In other words, the church did not just dominate the society: it *became* the society, the only society.

Knowledge, of course, is a crucial component of any society. The preservation of past learning, the teaching of that learning to new generations, and the development of new knowledge all constitute crucial aspects of what we would call civilization. Thus it is not surprising that the church permeated society especially by acting as the only viable social institution that stored, taught and extended knowledge. As one historian summarizes, "The moral and educational aspects continued through the work of bishops, cathedrals, monasteries, and parish churches."[51]

Monasteries played a particularly critical role in this process. Among the few stable places in an era drowned by invasions, plague and famine, the church's monasteries served as relatively tranquil arks crammed with knowledge. At their desks monks would pore over old texts—often the

---

[49]Brown, *World of Late Antiquity*, p. 15.
[50]Michael Novak, "Aquinas and the Heretics," *First Things*, December 1995, pp. 34, 57.
[51]Henry Mayr-Harting, quoted in *Oxford Illustrated History of Christianity*, ed. John McManners (Oxford: Oxford University Press, 1990), p. 108.

only extant copies in all of medieval Europe. Giles Constable has detailed
how this monastic editing and preservation of sacred texts marked "an
important step in the history of scholarship as well as of spirituality and
extended, in a tentative way, to legal and literary texts" all the way up to
the twelfth century.[52]

But monks did not remain completely cloistered with their texts. The
masses, lacking any system of secular schools, looked to these monasteries and their monks as the era's only classrooms and teachers. Thomas
Cahill, in his popular *How the Irish Saved Civilization*, has argued elo-
quently that monasteries in Ireland played an especially heroic role in
ensuring the survival of an educated civilization.[53] Whatever new art,
music and literature that emerged during the postimperial centuries similarly came from the church. To create these new works the church would
borrow—often heavily—raw cultural material from the remains of Roman
culture; but the collapse of the Roman culture itself meant that the
church alone shaped the final product.[54]

### The Epochal Story: The Only City

If the title of the epochal story in Augustine's era was "The Eternal
City," then the title for the story in Aquinas's is "The Only City." The
Only City story located knowledge solely in its environs: in its doctrines,
sacred texts, culture and institutions. As a metanarrative about the very
nature of knowledge, it was essentially a story in the philosophical
genre. For a character to become "one who knew," so the story went, he
or she would have to enter the Christian world. This is why when Count
Landolfo Aquinas wanted his son Thomas to gain an education, he sent
him to the great Benedictine monastery of Monte Cassino, even though

---

[52]Giles Constable, *The Reformation of the 12th Century* (Cambridge: Cambridge University
Press, 1996), p. 154. It would be interesting to trace the preservation of *City of God* itself
via these monastic "arks." It is most likely that the preservation of *COG* kept the memory
alive of many classical works which, while themselves lost to most of Europe, were mentioned in Augustine's critique.
[53]Thomas Cahill, *How the Irish Saved Civilization* (New York: Doubleday, 1995).
[54]In this process Augustine's legacy again played an important role. His *De doctrina christiana* was appropriated as a model of how Christians were to "take the spoils of the Egyp-
tians" and only use them to interpret Scripture—itself the sole basis of all Christian
learning.

by all accounts the father was not a devout man.[55] It is also no surprise that this epoch witnessed the founding of the great universities by the church. The Christian university embodied the Only City in its philosophical conviction that all truths were united within its walls.[56]

The philosophical narrative encompassed the search for knowledge of the highest object. If a character desired to know God himself, it was necessary to adopt not only Christian faith but also its accompanying culture. In the century following the final demise of the Empire, the prejudice that barbarians could never be filled with divine illumination (unless they were conquered by Rome) continued. It was not until the seventh century, under the leadership of the visionary Pope Gregory I, that Christian missions to the barbarian northern tribes of continental Europe began. Even then, missionaries persisted in viewing barbarians as "unlettered beasts" in need of the one true civilization.[57]

The alleged superiority of the western Christian civilization represented a crucial part of the missionary's rhetorical strategy with the barbarians. St. Boniface, one of the most prominent advocates of mission in the eighth century, recorded the advice commonly given to outgoing missionaries: bring lots of showy, gold-leafed books and argue that Christians "possess fertile lands, and provinces fruitful in wine and oil and abounding in other riches" while the barbarians languished in poverty.[58] Four centuries later, another missionary to the Pomeranians would receive a letter with similar advice: "If you, dear father, wish to make any gains in the brute hearts of these barbarians, you must go there with a noble retinue of companions and servants and a plentiful supply of food and clothing. Those who, with unbridled neck, despised the yoke of humility will bow their necks in reverence for the glory of riches."[59] Medieval missionaries in barbarian lands, like some of their nineteenth-century European descendants in Africa and Asia, practi-

---

[55]Ralph McInerny, *St. Thomas Aquinas* (Boston: Twayne, 1977), p. 13.
[56]Alasdair MacIntyre, *Three Rival Versions of Moral Enquiry* (Notre Dame, Ind.: University of Notre Dame Press, 1990), pp. 82-103.
[57]Markus, *Christianity in the Roman World*, pp. 179-84.
[58]Quoted in Fletcher, *Barbarian Conversion*, p. 242.
[59]Ibid., p. 458. For other examples, see pp. 120, 236-38, 516.

cally equated evangelism with the exaltation of their own culture.

This epochal story was a very self-enclosed narrative. Societies that describe themselves as the "only city" often risk extreme insularity. The China that declared itself the Middle Kingdom, after all, was the very one that constructed the Great Wall.[60] The inherited epoch of Aquinas conceived of its own learning and culture as so self-sufficient that it made no great attempt to engage seriously with others. Benjamin Kedar summarizes the reason:

> Catholic Europeans failed to concern themselves with Islam because of the very character of early medieval Latin culture. The concentration on Scripture and patristic writings and the dependence on the summaries of knowledge compiled in late antiquity led to an emulation or continuation of past efforts and achievements, leaving little scope for seriously tackling the post-Biblical, postclassical, postpatristic—and from this viewpoint inherently marginal—phenomenon of Islam.[61]

Consequently little intellectual work was directed toward even understanding the "inherently marginal phenomenon of Islam." Churchmen who even contemplated going on missions to these lands were dissuaded.[62] Missionaries like Ramon of Penyaforte who wrote to Aquinas for help were truly unusual.

### The Epochal Challenge: Another City

The reluctance to go to the Muslim lands was reinforced by the jarring effect such a meeting had on Christians. Islam simply did not fit very well into the story of the Only City. The story worked with the barbarian tribes to the north: such tribes had only local pagan rites and a limited culture to oppose the Christian proclamation. The seeming universalism and superior learning of the Christian faith often convinced barbarians to convert, thus reinforcing Catholic Europe's own faith in its epochal story.

---

[60]For an interesting analysis of the insulating tendency of a society that conceives of itself as "the only city" vis-à-vis "the uncultured barbarians," see Arthur Waldron, *The Great Wall of China* (Cambridge: Cambridge University Press, 1990).

[61]Benjamin Z. Kedar, *Crusade and Mission* (Princeton, N.J.: Princeton University Press, 1984), p. 41.

[62]Ibid., pp. 56, 84.

Muslims, however, were not so easily impressed. Unlike the pagan tribes, they self-consciously belonged to a worldwide religion. After Muhammad's death in Arabia in 632, the second caliph 'Umar led an amazing expansion of this nascent faith. In the span of one hundred years it spread westward to Egypt, along the North African coast (swallowing up the home of Augustine) and into Spain. Eastward, Islam toppled the enormous Sassanid (Persian) empire and dominated all of the ancient societies within it.[63] Geographically, it appeared to Islam (quite correctly) that it enclosed Christendom and not vice versa. The "marginal" suddenly demanded attention.

Moreover, Islam practiced a culture that was what postmodern scholars call "totalizing." The Qur'an enclosed Islamic society just as much as the Bible enclosed European society. For example, Muslim sources report that when the victorious Arab commander captured Alexandria, he asked 'Umar what ought to be done with its famous library. 'Umar allegedly replied, "If the books are in accordance with the Qur'an, they are unnecessary, and may be destroyed; if they contradict the Qur'an, they are dangerous and should certainly be destroyed."[64]

One of the key functions of Muslim religious scholars, the *ulema,* was to guard the laity from hearing any impugning of Islamic doctrines. Christian missionaries quickly found out that they incurred the *ulema*'s verdict of the death penalty if they conducted polemics against Islam.[65] This totalizing society felt no need to converse with Christianity.

Unsurprisingly, Christian missionaries who could conceive of only the rhetorical strategy they had employed for centuries against cowed, admiring barbarian tribes were baffled. Most tried to ignore the Islamic lands as long as possible. Instead they kept returning to the audiences that still listened to the old lines. So church leaders diverted missionary efforts to pagan tribes like the Danes, directly contrasting the ease of converting such pagans with the unfavorable prospects of converting Muslims. Kedar concludes: "Daunted by the Muslim interdiction, the Christians—Nestorians, Byzantines, and Catholic Europeans alike—chose the route of lesser

---

[63]William M. Watt, *Muslim-Christian Encounters* (London: Routledge, 1991), p. 59.
[64]Quoted in ibid., p. 41.
[65]Kedar, *Crusade and Mission,* p. 9.

resistance, dispatching missionaries to the less-refractory pagans of their respective norths and northeasts, where the danger seemed less and the past gains held the promise of future success."[66]

But Islam would not go away. It stared back at the West with the defiant features of a rival and self-sufficient worldview. Between West and East there seemed to only exist what Alasdair MacIntyre calls "extreme *incommensurability* and *untranslatability*." With no words to say and no authority to share, Christians reached for the sword to wield. Thus this epoch witnessed the Crusades, widely justified in the minds of contemporaries by the recalcitrance of Muslims to conversion.[67] The rare occasions of Muslim conversion usually occurred only after Christians militarily conquered a region. More extreme still, some Christians advocated forcible baptism and conversion, as evidenced by one of the most popular vernacular works of the epoch, the *Song of Roland*. Even Christian thinkers like theologian Johannes Duns Scotus would advocate such practices.[68]

### The Challengers' Story: The Aristotelian Story of Knowledge

Islam did not just resist Christianity; it also directly threatened its epochal story. The philosophical blade of the scimitar flashed most brilliantly in the form of Aristotle. The Aristotelian framework challenged the Only City philosophical story that a person must enter the Christian world to gain knowledge, especially the knowledge of God.

The works of Aristotle had been lost to the West for centuries but were preserved in the East via the Sassanid empire. When Islam conquered those regions in the eighth century, it also discovered Aristotle. Aristotelian thought came to provide the basis for Arabic learning in fields ranging from mathematics to astronomy to architecture.[69] Aristotelian science, emphasizing the sensory-based observations of the Actual, quickly produced superior findings to Western science, which was still based on the Platonic contemplation of the Ideal.[70] Ironically, the crusades forced

---

[66]Ibid., p. 14.
[67]See ibid., chap. 2.
[68]Ibid., pp. 68, 187.
[69]Watt, *Muslim-Christian Encounters*, p. 55.
[70]See MacIntyre, *Three Rival Versions*, pp. 105-26

Christians to confront this superiority in learning. For instance, when Christian soldiers captured Sevilla in 1248, they were "amazed at the grandeur, luxury, refinement and beauty of a city superior in so many ways to the towns they were familiar with."[71] Western scholars began to stream to other captured cities such as Toledo to learn from Muslim intellectuals still living there.[72] Suddenly it seemed that to be truly educated one had to leave the Christian world and enter the Muslim one.

Christians would initially try to finesse their way out of this challenge. The first Western scholars who returned to Europe with this new learning invariably described the import as "Arabic" rather than "Islamic" learning.[73] But such flimsy tactics gave way when the philosophical story itself crashed into the West. A highly influential school of Islamic philosophical theology, the Falasifa, had been wrestling with the texts of Aristotle for centuries. The greatest of the Falasifa, Avicenna (d. 1037) and Averroës (d. 1198), produced prodigious commentaries on Aristotle. Although these men caused controversy among their own coreligionists, they were undeniably Islamic. Averroës, for example, was an eminent *qadi*, a religious judge. During the twelfth century in Spain, huge numbers of these philosophical commentaries were translated from Arabic into Latin and flooded into Christendom. One scholar comments on the effect: "[Aristotelian philosophy] had been known largely by hearsay for centuries, snippets culled from the Fathers, some few books on Aristotelian logic. . . . Suddenly, as it must have seemed, a vast library of erudition drops from the heavens. What to make of it was an understandably pressing matter."[74] As Chesterton puts it, the fact that this was an Islamic challenge could not be avoided: "The panic upon the Aristotelian peril, that had passed across the high places of the Church . . . was really filled rather with fear of Mahomet."[75]

This "vast library of erudition" dropping from the Muslim heavens

[71]Watt, *Muslim-Christian Encounters*, p. 83.

[72]Ibid., p. 56.

[73]Kedar, *Crusade and Mission*, p. 90.

[74]Ralph McInerny, *A First Glance at St. Thomas Aquinas* (Notre Dame, Ind.: University of Notre Dame Press, 1990), p. 44.

[75]G. K. Chesterton, *Saint Thomas Aquinas* (New York: Doubleday, 1956), p. 84.

threatened to topple the Only City claim that one had to adopt Christianity and Christian learning to know God. The reader who flipped through newly received pages of Avicenna and Averroës would find a well-reasoned and articulated path to divine illumination that was totally independent of Christian culture.[76]

This Aristotelian story seemed flatly opposed to the Christian one in some key features, especially its characterization of God and humankind. For example, the beginning of the story was different: Islamic commentators interpreted Aristotle's proof of the Prime Mover ("that the realm of mobile being has always been") to mean that the world has always existed, contradicting the Bible's opening characterization of God as Creator. The Falasifa also read Aristotle to mean that humankind lacks personal immortality. This denial sharply challenged the medieval European emphasis on an individual's future as a soul forever united with God in heaven. Finally, the commentators presented Aristotle as questioning the Christian doctrine of providence. Aristotle, in their interpretation, depicted God as "thought thinking itself," strongly suggesting that God is basically unconcerned with the world and in fact does not personally know or direct what happens to human beings.[77]

Thus the philosophical story of Aristotle fundamentally challenged the inherited epoch. Allied with Islam, it was a radically different story of knowledge that presented rather disturbing characterizations of God and humanity. Into this clash would step Thomas Aquinas and his *Summa contra Gentiles*.

### Aquinas: Bilingual and On the Margins

Like Augustine, Thomas Aquinas seems to have been especially prepared for this challenge by his personal history. Like Augustine, Aquinas bene-

---

[76]Note that centuries earlier some orthodox Muslim readers of Averroës and Avicenna felt a similar fear that Aristotle invalidated the claims of the Qur'an. See Watt, *Muslim-Christian Encounters*, p. 55. I am of course not claiming that the Aristotelian story sums up Islam itself; rather, I am saying that the Aristotelian metanarrative sums up the philosophical challenge Islam presented to Western Christendom.

[77]See McInerny, *St. Thomas Aquinas*, p. 31-32, for the summary of these philosophical challenges.

fited from a thoroughly "bilingual" education and yet also located himself on the margins of the epoch.

Thomas's early education very much fit the standard pattern of his epoch. His early education took place at Monte Cassino, one of the greatest monasteries of the day. He studied at the University of Paris, one of the newly established universities which claimed to unite all learning within its walls. His earliest works reflected the self-enclosed clerical culture described above. Before *Summa contra Gentiles*, he had only written commentaries on different parts of Scripture, a commentary on the *Sentences* by Peter Lombard and two theological tracts on Boethius—all standard exercises for that era's intellectuals.[78] He would study and teach in Paris, Cologne and the papal curia—all centers of that era's learning.

Indeed the Aquinas of popular imagination has been tagged as a figure cloistered within the Christian world. But in reality Aquinas was unusually exposed to the world outside the insular Christian culture. He grew up in the province of Aquino in Naples, part of the kingdom of Sicily. This region, one historian notes, "reflected the face of Europe turned to the Islamicate, as evidenced in [a passage from] the first translations commissioned from Arabic: 'Latin, Muslim, and Jewish culture mingled freely in Sicily in a unique way that was peculiarly Sicilian.' "[79] This pluralistic setting was probably the one in which he composed a good portion of *Summa contra Gentiles*.[80] Moreover, Sicily had in the twelfth century witnessed an unusual number of Muslim conversions.[81] Aquinas was second cousin to Frederick II, whose local army included Muslim soldiers and whose court supported Muslim scholars.[82] This region, with all its tumbling intellectual diversity, clearly held an attraction for Aquinas. Years later when he was asked to direct a theological *studium*, he

---

[78]See Pegis, introduction to *SCG* 1, pp. 15-16.

[79]David B. Burrell, "Aquinas and Islamic and Jewish Thinkers," in *The Cambridge Companion to Aquinas*, ed. Norman Kretzmann and Eleonore Stump (Cambridge: Cambridge University Press, 1993), p. 62.

[80]Norman Kretzmann, "Thomas Aquinas," in *Routledge Encyclopedia of Philosophy* (London: Routledge, 1998), 1:329.

[81]Kedar, *Crusade and Mission*, p. 51.

[82]James Waltz, "Muhammad and the Muslims in St. Thomas Aquinas," *The Muslim World* 66 (April 1976): 87.

expressly chose to establish one in Naples rather than in a more standard locale such as Rome, Orvieto or Paris.[83]

Most important, in addition to his standard education Aquinas consciously sought out a "bilingual" education. He studied at the University of Naples, the Western institution of higher learning that had probably received the most Islamic scholarship of all the universities.[84] Aquinas also repeatedly pursued relationships with figures who already were unusually fluent in the challengers' terms. After graduating from the University of Naples, Aquinas traveled to study under Albert the Great. Albert was a Western pioneer in the practice of science under the Aristotelian framework. He was also one of the foremost authorities on the Islamic commentaries flooding in at that time and was most likely responsible for directing Aquinas's attention towards Avicenna and Averroës.[85] Aquinas also would come into contact with the works of Peter of Cluny, who a few decades earlier had translated portions of the Qur'an and summarized Islamic belief.[86] Finally, Aquinas benefited from a network of relationships with fellow Dominicans like Ramon of Penyaforte and William of Moerbeke. Moerbeke would revise older translations of Aristotle and provide Aquinas with his first translations of the philosopher directly from the Greek.[87]

Aquinas's relationships with these Dominicans also illustrate the fruitful consequences of his most radical decision to locate himself on the margins of his epoch. He had been born into a noble family which was very influential in the church's attempt to establish itself as the defining social force of Sicily. Two of his brothers had fought for the pope. His father had originally sent him to Mt. Cassino in the hope that he would be appointed to the powerful position of abbot in that monastery. By all accounts, Thomas had a promising future. However, at the age of nineteen he shocked everyone by choosing to take monastic vows and join the

[83]Burrell, "Aquinas and Islamic and Jewish Thinkers," p. 62.

[84]Waltz, "Muhammad and the Muslims," p. 87.

[85]Chesterton, *Saint Thomas Aquinas*, pp. 66-71.

[86]Waltz, "Muhammad and the Muslims," pp. 88-89.

[87]Jan A. Aertsen, "Aquinas's Philosophy in Its Historical Setting," in *The Cambridge Companion to Aquinas*, ed. Norman Kretzmann and Eleonore Stump (Cambridge: Cambridge University Press, 1993), p. 21.

Dominicans, one of the new mendicant movements.[88] It was a pattern he would repeat throughout his life. Years later he would even reject a papal offer to be appointed archbishop in order to continue as a lowly Dominican friar.

The Dominicans, like other mendicant movements formed in that day, operated very much at the fringe of the epoch. Their vows of poverty rang out as an implicit critique of the Only City's conflation of social power with the church. Unlike other monks, the mendicants relied for their upkeep not on vast real estate holdings but on begging.[89] The Dominicans also were the first religious order founded expressly for preaching and the training of preachers. In their relation to Islam these preachers represented a new voice calling out in the wilderness. They were among the few voices mounting any sort of critique of the crusades while most of the society rushed to this option.[90] Mendicant Francis of Assisi first pointed to an alternative by taking the unprecedented step of crossing crusader battle lines to preach to the Muslims.[91] Dominic, the founder of Thomas's order, had himself at one time planned to go to the Muslim lands to preach. Dominic's bishop, Diego of Osma (whom many consider to be the initiator of the Dominican method), also tried to resign his high offices so that he might be "free to preach the gospel to Muslims."[92] When Thomas was eight years old, the Dominicans took the unconventional step of seeking permission from Frederick II to evangelize Lucera, a colony of Sicilian Muslims near Thomas's hometown.[93] It is interesting to speculate whether the memory of this attempt influenced Thomas to join the order some years later.

Aquinas wrote almost nothing that dealt directly with the crusades—not surprising given that he avoided explicit discussion of almost any contemporary issue. While he never condemned the crusades outright,

---

[88]John Finnis, *Aquinas* (Oxford: Oxford University Press, 1998), pp. 2-7.

[89]For an excellent historical overview of the mendicant movement and its location on the periphery of the epoch, see Constable, *Reformation of the 12th Century*.

[90]See Kedar, *Crusade and Mission*, chap. 3.

[91]Ibid., p. 119. See also p. 124 for how St. Francis included in his rule of Friars Minor a chapter dealing specifically with missionary work among the Muslims.

[92]Ibid., p. 120.

[93]Ibid., p. 137.

his writing includes a brief but clear rejection of the forcible conversion of Muslims.[94] Louder than his words, though, his unflagging commitment to his order testified to his desire for an alternative to force. Ramon of Penyaforte heard enough of Aquinas's desire to correspond with him about a rhetorical strategy for his missionaries.

Aquinas's commitment to a life lived on the margins was tested from the beginning. When told of his decision to join the Dominicans, his older brothers—at least one of whom actually fought in a crusade—were so enraged that they forcibly abducted him while he was traveling toward Paris with a group of senior Dominicans. The kidnappers took him to a remote castle and declared they would keep him imprisoned until he recanted. He refused. For over a year the teenager waited out his older captors. Legend has it that he used his time in prison fruitfully memorizing much of the Bible and other scholarly literature that would eventually find its way into works like *Summa contra Gentiles*. Eventually his brothers gave up and released him. Thomas placidly resumed his journey.[95]

Contemporaries of Thomas Aquinas describe him as a large, heavy-set figure who plodded about rather slowly and silently. When he was studying under Albert the Great, his fellow pupils derisively called him the Dumb Ox. But this giant of a thinker consistently and deliberately followed less-trodden paths. He fulfilled the prophecy of Albert his teacher, who proclaimed to his other pupils, "You call him a Dumb Ox; I tell you this Dumb Ox shall bellow so loud that his bellowings will fill the world."[96]

### Summary of the Historical Comparison

Both *City of God* and *Summa contra Gentiles* are works forged in the heat of conflict. They stand amidst the confrontation of rival epochal stories. In Augustine's day pagan challengers sought to deconstruct the Eter-

---

[94]Ibid., p. 187. Out of the thousands of pages that Aquinas wrote, scholar John Finnis can locate only a few scattered lines that deal with various personal moral questions in which the Crusades play a rather incidental role. Finnis notes that Aquinas does have a sentence acknowledging the possibility of a religious society established to fight to reclaim the Holy Lands. See Finnis, *Aquinas*, p. 15.

[95]Finnis, *Aquinas*, p. 6.

[96]Chesterton, *Saint Thomas Aquinas*, p. 71.

nal City narrative by blaming Christianity for Rome's ills. The challenge consisted of the three subplots of political, religious and philosophical history. If unmet, this rival story would lead audiences into a post-Christian worldview. In Aquinas's day, Islam threatened the Only City narrative by presenting a totally different and seemingly superior story of knowledge. The philosophical challenge assumed its sharpest form in the Aristotelian narrative of knowledge—especially knowledge of God himself—and its characterizations of God and humankind. If unanswered, this opposing narrative would draw listeners into the paralyzing relativism so common to religious pluralism.

Both authors were remarkably prepared to enter the fray. Both received excellent training in their challengers' language as well as that of their own inherited epoch. Yet both also wrote from the margins, where they could command a certain independent perspective.

Their "bilingual" training and independent perspective would shape their angular responses in *City of God* and *Summa contra Gentiles*. As the next two chapters seek to detail, both works brilliantly execute the strategy of "taking every thought captive." They enter the challengers' story on the challengers' own terms. Then they retell a modified rendition, using the story's own language. Finally, they tell their own larger metanarrative, custom designed to capture the corrected tale. These metanarratives, which are crafted versions of the gospel story, do not slavishly repeat the epochal story they inherited. They tell a new story for a new day.

# Engaging a Post-Christian Society

## City of God

As a response to the challengers' story, *City of God* is itself a massive story. The strategy of "taking every thought captive" by definition requires something of an epic: a metanarrative that contains stories within its story. Such an epic usually weaves its overarching plot with various subplots in a carefully constructed manner. Thus before plunging into a detailed analysis of Augustine's strategy in this complex work, it will be helpful to gain an overview of *City of God*. In particular, it is important to understand *City of God*'s basic structure, genre and central dramatic action.

### Structure

The overall organization of *City of God* follows the three components of the strategy: enter, retell and capture. The first two components involve working within the challengers' story, while the third marks a shift into the gospel metanarrative. Augustine consciously structured his work to reflect this shift. When he completed the manuscript, he wrote to his original publisher with deliberate instructions that the finished product should be divided into two volumes: books 1-10 in volume 1 and books 11-22 in volume 2.[1]

Volume 1 relies almost exclusively on pagan sources. It is a tour de force of classical learning: there are hundreds of citations from the dozens of ancient texts that served as the authorities of the pagan challengers' story. This is the material that Augustine simultaneously enters and reinterprets.

In his transition into volume 2, Augustine explains he is shifting to his metanarrative: "But we have already replied to the enemies of this Holy City, in the first ten books, to the best of our ability, with the assistance of our Lord and King. And now . . . my task is to discuss, to the best of my power, the rise, the development, and the destined ends of the two cities, the earthly and the heavenly."[2] His grand story of two cities—the heavenly "city of God" and the earthly "city of men"—serves as his means of capturing the pagan challenge. The source material for volume 2 shifts accordingly. Volume 2 is mostly composed of biblical material covering these two cities' prehistorical origins, their developments through history and finally their ultimate destinations at the end of history. Augustine works in some secular material (mostly in books 18-19) on the "city of men" in such a way that the two cities represent two strands in an intertwined story. Volume 2 essentially weaves them into a narrative net that will encompass the challengers.

### Genre

*City of God* assumes the historical genre for the obvious reason that the challengers' story came in three historical subplots of Roman politics, religion and philosophy. The challengers sought to deconstruct the historical events surrounding the fall of Rome to reveal Christianity as the evil culprit. Since the pagans had picked the field of history to do battle, Augustine chose to meet them there.

As noted in chapter one, scholars have debated the basic genre of *City of God*, questioning whether it is in essence a theological or a philosophi-

---

[1] We are very fortunate that this letter was discovered in 1939 by a Benedictine scholar. See O'Meara, introduction to *COG*, p. xxxvi
[2] *COG* 11.1, pp. 429-30

cal work. Yet the overwhelming bulk of Augustine's material is historical. Certainly he engages in philosophical or theological argument at times, but he does so mainly to guard key sections of his historical net from tearing. For instance, he engages in a philosophical analysis of the supreme end of life, but with the ultimate purpose of clarifying the eschaton, the very conclusion of history.[3] Elsewhere he undertakes a philosophical examination of rational proof in order to show that the miraculous events of his narrative could really have happened.[4] Augustine takes such pains to demonstrate that his gospel metanarrative is actually true, not merely what postmoderns call a "socially constructed" tale. His theological discussion of scriptural interpretation is aimed at reinforcing this key point that "we also believe in *the truth of the story* as a faithful record of historical fact."[5]

While history is important to his strategy of response, Augustine also chooses the genre for a more profound reason. *City of God* is a work written by a man convinced that his God is the God of history: "He gives in accordance with the order of events in history. . . . Yet God is not bound in subjection to this order of events; he is himself in control, as the master of events, and arranges the order of things as a governor."[6] Augustine employs his powers of philosophical argument to debunk any notion of history as captive to superstition, astrology, fortune or any other force but God.[7]

This God has also communicated "the mystery of eternal life" to human beings throughout history: "It [the mystery] was revealed to those who were fit to receive the knowledge by means of signs and symbols appropriate to the times."[8] Therefore Christians living in space and time must pay close attention to history and historical epochs:

> The experience of mankind in general, as far as God's people is concerned, is comparable to the experience of the individual man. There is a process

---

[3]*COG* 18.54, p. 841.
[4]*COG* 21.5, p. 971, and 22.8, pp. 1033-43.
[5]*COG* 13.22, p. 535.
[6]*COG* 4.34, p. 176, emphasis mine
[7]*COG* 5.8-9, pp. 189-92.
[8]*COG* 7.32, p. 293

of education, through the epochs of a people's history, as through the successive stages of a man's life, designed to raise them from the temporal and the visible to an apprehension of the eternal and invisible.[9]

Because God has so communicated via history, the Christian who engages with another people group must attend to the epochs of a people's history in order to hear the divine Teacher's lesson plan for them. The Christian's attention span must cover more than the immediate era, because "through his created beings [God] spoke in successive syllables, following one another in transitory intervals of time."[10] By digging through a people's historical past, the Christian can piece together successive syllables to form the prequel to God's word to them today.

It follows that no people group needs to abandon its history. All peoples can properly claim that their past contains divinely composed preparations for the gospel. The historical nature of Christ authorizes this reverence for history. Christ entered human history and "disclosed openly what in previous ages had been indicated by veiled allusions, when hints were given in accordance with the stages of mankind's development, following the plan decided upon by God, in his wisdom."[11]

The implications for a missionary are obvious. The preservation of all historical stories—even the most marginal, the most pagan—is a missiological enterprise of the highest order. The obliteration of tribal narratives by European missionaries is to be lamented by the church even more than by postmodern critics. Who knows how many of God's hints were ignored in the process? Who knows how much of our currently proclaimed word remains incoherent, awaiting the retrieval of some forgotten "syllable" to fill in the blanks?

In other words, *all* history is holy ground. For history is not just the genre of the book *City of God* but the genre of God himself. Therefore it will be absolutely crucial for Augustine to make evident God's complete possession of the field.

---

[9]*COG* 10.14, p. 392.
[10]*COG* 10.15, p. 393.
[11]*COG* 10.32, pp. 423-24.

## Central Dramatic Action

A long, complex epic can be helpfully summarized by its "central dramatic action." The best epic plots are defined by an overarching thematic action. For instance, the Arthurian Holy Grail legends can be summed up as "search," Victor Hugo's *Les Miserables* as "sacrifice," Charles Dickens's *Nicholas Nickleby* as "mature." The central dramatic action should be powerful enough to drive the entire plot along. Furthermore, the action will be repeated over and over as a motif throughout the story.

The central dramatic action of *City of God* can be aptly labeled "unveil." History itself is a series of "veiled allusions" that require disclosure and interpretation. More centrally, the plot of the metanarrative in volume 2 is driven by the act of unveiling the city of God and the city of men. The former represents the people devoted to God, the latter those who are devoted to themselves. The two cities are mixed together at birth. As they grow up they are still "interwoven, as it were, in this transitory world, and mingled with one another."[12] But Augustine as narrator will unveil them in his telling of the story "so that my readers may observe both cities and mark the contrast between them."[13] The definitive act of unveiling will take place, as most central dramatic actions do, at the climax of the narrative. As in *The Prince and the Pauper*, *Twelfth Night* and countless other works, this plot will take twins whose identities are disguised and bring them to their ultimate revelation.

The act of unveiling is closely related to the act of retelling. What has long been mixed up is finally clarified. In the final two books of volume 2 Augustine describes a moment when all historical episodes will be reinterpreted and represented in the correct light. The wicked and the righteous will be made distinct, so distinct that that they will take separate paths. The imagery of "taking right roads" and "false paths" dominates Augustine's literary repertoire throughout the entire work. A visual picture of the plot of *City of God* might look like a long road that finally forks only near the end.[14]

While the most decisive unveiling takes place at the end, this action is

[12]*COG* 11.1, p. 430.
[13]*COG* 18.1, p. 762. See also 18.47, p. 829.
[14]See *COG* 10.29, p. 414; 10.32, p. 424; 11.2, p. 431; and 21.1- 22.30, pp. 964-1091.

woven into the epic from the beginning. In volume 1 Augustine enters the pagan challengers' story and retells it by unmasking its true nature.

## Entering and Retelling the Challengers' Story

In volume 1 Augustine simultaneously undertakes the first two steps of entering and retelling the challengers' story. The volume itself is divided neatly according to the three subplots of that story: books 1-5, books 6-7 and books 9-10 represent, respectively, forays into the political history, the religious history and the philosophical history of Rome.

*The subplot of Rome's politics.* Augustine opens his treatment of Rome's politics at a natural point of entry: Virgil's *Aeneid*, which chronicles the founding of the city and sets up its eternal destiny. Augustine quickly establishes common ground by lavishing loving attention on this pagan authority: "Virgil certainly is held to be a great poet; in fact he is regarded as the best and the most renowned of all poets, and for that reason he is read by children at an early age."[15] In the first five books he thoroughly utilizes the terms that Virgil provides. He cites the poet over seventy times, exceeding most of his pagan challengers' own use of Virgil.[16] Augustine seems to go out of his way to reassure pagans that his purpose is not to eradicate their sacred texts.

But he will also show that he reads those texts more closely than they do. Early on he cites Virgil's account of the fall of Troy, which prefaces Aeneas's refugee journey to Rome. Virgil's own words attribute the fall of Troy to the fact that Troy's gods are "vanquished." Augustine points out that Virgil's narrative links this preface with Rome's own opening act: before Aeneas leaves Troy to establish Rome, the hero is told, "To thee, Troy now entrusts her native gods."[17] Augustine of course does not believe in any of these gods,[18] but he will pose his question in their terms: "Was it really prudent to entrust the defence of Rome to the gods of Illium, after the lesson provided by the fate of Troy itself?"[19] Furthermore, if the gods

---

[15]*COG* 1.3, p. 8.
[16]O'Meara, introduction to *COG*, p. xxiii
[17]*COG* 1.3, p. 9.
[18]See *COG* 3.4, p. 92.
[19]*COG* 3.8, p. 96.

that were given to Aeneas had already been vanquished, how can the pagans claim Rome fell because Christianity removed those gods? They were already dead and defeated before Rome's beginning!

Since the challengers' narrative of Rome's fall does not cohere, Augustine feels free to provide a reinterpretation, while still relying on the challengers' own sources: "In fact, the only possible cause of destruction [of Rome in 410] was the choice of such perishable defenders. When the poets wrote and sang of 'vanquished gods,' it was not because it suited their whim to lie—they were men of sense, and truth compelled them to admit the facts."[20] Rome's own historical poets testify that Rome chose already fallen divinities and should only blame itself for its fall.

Elsewhere Augustine responds to the pagan accusation that the events of 410 provided historical evidence for the Christian God's untrustworthiness as the guardian of Rome's destiny. He again invites his challengers to examine their own history. He proceeds to list one ancient disaster after another that befell Rome, all before the introduction of Christianity.[21] He concludes his survey: "How can our opponents have the effrontery, the audacity, the impudence, the imbecility (or rather the insanity) to refuse to blame their gods for those catastrophes, while they hold Christ responsible for the disasters of modern times?"[22]

Far from demonstrating the Christian God's untrustworthiness, the pagans' own story can be retold as a verdict on their own gods. Augustine plumbs Roman historians Livy and Sallust to show "that the Roman divinities, when Scipio had defended their temples from Hannibal, did not defend him in return—though the only reason for their worship is to secure that kind of temporal blessing."[23] Rome's borders had likewise shrunk in the times before Christ, despite promises of the pagan gods' assistance.[24]

Augustine exposes other inconsistencies in the challengers' story. He examines the pagan intellectuals' agenda of blaming Christianity for all of

---

[20]*COG* 1.3, p. 9.
[21]*COG* 3.21-31, pp. 122-34.
[22]*COG* 3.30, p. 131.
[23]*COG* 3.21, p. 122.
[24]*COG* 4.29, p. 171.

Rome's internal social ills: "I am still dealing with the ignorant, the people whose stupidity has given rise to the popular proverb, 'No rain! It's all the fault of the Christians.' The well-educated who are fond of history . . . wish to inflame the hatred of the illiterate mobs against us."[25] But he then cites a breathtaking range of pagan historical authorities, ranging from Cicero to Sallust back to Virgil, to show that many of these very ills were rampant long before Christianity arrived on the scene.[26]

Augustine retells the pagan story to uncover the very heart of Rome's politics. The pagan story had claimed that the novelty of Christianity violated Rome's essence: Rome's very identity as a *civitas* depended on its continuity with its glorious past. Augustine claims that the deepest identity of a city stems not from its historical continuity but from its moral continuity. Justice, even pagans will agree, is the essence of a commonwealth. "Remove justice," he reminds his reader, "and what are kingdoms but gangs of criminals on a large scale? What are criminal gangs but petty kingdoms?"[27] In book 5 he proceeds to compile his most impressive collection yet of pagan historical sources. He proclaims the results of his survey: underneath Rome's rhetoric of justice was simply "the love of domination, the greed for praise and glory."[28] Rome's underlying love of domination and greed for praise and glory recur over and over in Augustine's work.[29] Rome was never a true city because it was never just—even in its "glorious" past.

Note that in unveiling Rome's history as a story of "love of domination," Augustine anticipates one of postmodernism's most pressing claims. In the nineteenth century Nietzsche claimed a breakthrough discovery when he showed that his European society's moral claims and notions of universal justice actually covered up a raw "will to power." But he was merely repeating the same insight Augustine had already made fourteen hundred years earlier—except that Augustine had tackled an arguably more totalizing civilization and had certainly employed better historical evidence.

---

[25]*COG* 2.3, p. 50. See also 3.31, p. 133.
[26]*COG* 2.3, p. 50; 2.21, p. 72; 2.22, p. 75; and 3.20-31, pp. 119-34.
[27]*COG* 4.4, p. 139.
[28]*COG* 5.12, p. 197
[29]For example, see *COG* 4, pp 135-78, as well as 5 15, p. 204; and 5.20, p. 215

Augustine relentlessly deconstructs other aspects of Rome's political pretensions. For example, Rome had long claimed that its political power derived from the virtue of its devoted preservation of ancient rites. Augustine seizes this "covering story" of virtue and refashions it to explain Rome with greater candor than Rome is willing to offer. He argues that pagans actually demand such worship to exercise further political domination:

> The leaders of men (who were not men of integrity, but the human counterparts of the demons) taught men as true, under the name of religion, things they knew to be false. By this means they bound them tighter, as it were, to the citizen community, so that they might bring them under control and keep them there by the same technique. What chance had a weak and ignorant individual of escaping from the deceits of the statesmen and the demons?[30]

In passages like this Augustine again presents a political analysis that was stunningly original for its time and for centuries to come. He takes apart an entire civilization's ideologies to reveal them as masks for raw power. Once again, today's postmoderns can only claim to be descendants of this ancient master. Before Antonio Gramsci coined the term "ideological hegemony" to describe how the powerful shape popular belief for their own ends, before Michel Foucault claimed to have revealed previously unsuspected tools of oppression, this masterpiece of political deconstruction had been sitting on shelves for over a millennium.[31]

*The subplot of Rome's religion.* As in the realm of politics, Augustine reveals the internal inconsistencies in the pagan religious rites. For example, he playfully points out that the pagans cannot even get straight which gods are actually the ones in charge of Rome.[32] But his most interesting moves surround his textual analysis of the works of Marcus Varro.

---

[30]*COG* 4.32, p. 176.
[31]Antonio Gramsci, *Selections from the Prison Notebooks* (New York: International Publishers, 1989), pp. 416-18. For an excellent example of the postmodern's unveiling of such tools, see Michel Foucault, *Discipline and Punish* (New York: Vintage, 1979). For a fascinating example of how Augustine prefigures the postmodern historian's claim that "truth belongs to the bigger battalions," see *COG* 4.4, p. 139, where Augustine tells the story of a pirate who claims as much legitimacy as Alexander the Great.
[32]*COG* 3.5, p. 92; 4.24-25, p. 166.

As he did with Virgil, Augustine commends this renowned pagan historian of religion: "Has anyone pursued research in this subject further than Marcus Varro? Who has made more scholarly discoveries, or pondered the facts more assiduously? Who has made nicer distinctions, or written more carefully or more fully on those matters?"[33] With such affirmations Augustine communicates to his challengers that he accepts Varro as the shared authority on the topic of pagan religion.

But while Varro's texts guide Augustine's exploration of the pagan temple, he does not read them uncritically. Augustine's textual examination of Varro once again earns him the title "the original postmodern."

Postmodern literary critics claim to be able to dispense with the conscious intentions of an author by doing a "deep reading" of how ideas are organized within the text. To take a simple example, a postmodern critic might point out that in the Chronicles of Narnia C. S. Lewis consistently conveys the idea of purity with the word *white* while conveying impurity with the word *black*. This parallel structure, according to the critic, reveals Westerners' claims of racial superiority. The critic may attempt an even deeper reading and argue that the text's constant pairing of *purity* and *impurity* reveals a deeper commonality between the two concepts, a commonality that may even escape Lewis the author. Deep down, perhaps even in Lewis's subconscious, there is no difference between these concepts, but he nevertheless must make up an arbitrary moral distinction in order to separate out a racial group different from his own. Even if Lewis protested, "But that's not what I meant!" the postmodern feels quite confident in revealing intentions counter to the author's stated ones.[34]

Augustine subjects Varro to this same scrutiny. He seizes on how Varro sets up a parallel structure between "human matters" and "divine matters" and claims that this textual feature reveals a deeper similarity

---

[33]*COG* 6.2, p. 229.

[34]For some examples of such readings see Ellen Armour, *Deconstruction, Feminist Theology and the Problem of Difference* (Chicago: University of Chicago Press, 1999); Doreen Fowler, *Faulkner: The Return of the Repressed* (Charlottesville: University Press of Virginia, 1997). For a helpful overview of the nuances within postmodern literary theories, see Grant Osborne, *The Hermeneutical Spiral* (Downers Grove, Ill.: InterVarsity Press, 1991), pp. 367-415.

between the two. Moreover, the fact that Varro consistently gives precedence to human matters reveals Varro's subconscious belief about the true origin of divine matters. "Truth cries out, without need of a word from Varro," that the pagan divinities are simply human inventions.[35] Pagan religion, in the words of some postmodern scholars of religion, is simply "the sacred canopy" over "the social construction of reality."[36]

Augustine then turns to Varro's literary distinction between "civil gods," which supposedly ought to be venerated by the community, and "fabulous gods," which Varro admits are simply human fictions created for fabulous shows at public theaters. A closer analysis of the etymology and mythology of these supposedly distinct gods, according to Augustine, reveals that the two types are actually one and the same.[37] Therefore the distinction is removed and Varro's admission regarding the fabulous gods applies to both regardless of the author's intention: "But, whether you like it or not, some of your shots land on the 'civil' gods as well."[38]

In deconstructing Varro's distinctions, Augustine claims superior insight into the text: "So let our friends go and try (and good luck to them!) to use all their subtlety to make a distinction between 'civil' and 'fabulous' theology . . . between what is to be desired and what is to be rejected. *We understand what they are up to*."[39] What Varro and "they" are really "up to" is trying to conceal the truth that these pagan gods are socially constructed fictions. Again Augustine asserts that Varro's own literary devices give him away: "You yourself feel, when you consider them [the pagan gods] in all their aspects, that they are utterly alien from the nature of the gods . . . and the whole of your literature is loud in condemnation of them."[40]

Yet even while unmasking Varro's words so thoroughly, Augustine is not without sympathy for Varro himself. He still compliments Varro's eru-

---

[35]*COG* 6.4, p. 233.
[36]Peter Berger, *The Sacred Canopy: Elements of a Sociological Theory of Religion* (Garden City, N.Y.: Doubleday, 1967); Peter Berger and Thomas Luckmann, *The Social Construction of Reality* (Garden City, N.Y.: Doubleday, 1966).
[37]*COG* 6.6-9, pp. 236-48.
[38]*COG* 6.6, p. 237.
[39]*COG* 6.9, p. 246, emphasis mine
[40]*COG* 6.6, p. 236.

dition and dedication to the subject matter. Augustine does not depict the author as a malignant figure. Instead he portrays Varro as a person motivated by a very human (and postmodern) fear: the fear of being marginalized. "You are only a man," Augustine sighs, ". . . you are afraid of falling foul of pernicious popular notions and traditional practices in state-established superstitions."[41]

In Augustine's rendition, Varro becomes a tragic figure. Varro must go along with the massive state-established coverup; "since he found himself in a community already ancient, the only course open to him was to conform to its traditional ways." Augustine argues that if Varro had been able to form his own ideal community, he would not have to cower in fear of being marginalized. He could have been free to more honestly express the true nature of the Roman gods.[42] Augustine thus recharacterizes Varro, turning a would-be opponent almost into a potential partner in *City of God's* investigation of pagan religion.

The "coverup" is a common motif in our current epoch. The fascination with alleged plots to conceal UFO landings or the true assassin of JFK bears witness to a general distrust of governing institutions. Yet in the many popular movies like *All the President's Men* that tell some version of the coverup story, we consistently meet a "Deep Throat" character, a fearful but sympathetic figure who struggles with his or her own part in the larger conspiracy. Like Augustine's recharacterized Varro, this figure gives out veiled hints of a darker reality. In the stock scene that has almost become a cliché, this person whispers ominously to the investigating hero, "You don't know what you're up against! You don't know how deep it goes!"

If I may be permitted a brief deconstructionist reading, I believe these scenes reveal the postmodern subconscious sense that indeed "it" goes far deeper than what was previously thought. Movies of our epoch are permeated by what postmoderns call a "hermeneutic of suspicion"—only this suspicion evokes inchoate fears that deep down there lurks something even more supernaturally menacing than human figures or

---

[41]*COG* 6.6, p. 236.
[42]*COG* 6.4, pp. 233-34

even human institutions. As the apostle Paul put it, "Our struggle is not against enemies of blood and flesh" (Eph 6:12). It is striking how often, compared to even twenty-five years ago, this fear now dominates our cinema. Horror movies like *The Exorcist, Poltergeist* or just about any Stephen King-based film all play on disquieting fears that underneath everyday human experience lies primordial evil.

Augustine shares this suspicion about Rome. He concludes his retelling of the city's religious story by pulling back its last veil. Once again, its own historians will supply the raw material for his exposé:

> There is no difficulty in discovering the methods of pagan worship: we can easily see its infamy and degradation. But it would be hard to discover what, or whom, they worship if their own historians did not bear witness that the performances, which they admit to be foully obscene, were offered to powers who demanded such worship with terrible menaces. Hence it is clear, without any ambiguity, that this "civil" theology has invited wicked demons and unclean spirits to take up residence in those senseless images and by this means to gain possession of the hearts of the stupid.[43]

Augustine traces how demons in fact were behind Rome's historical origin: "When I speak of the miracles of the gods of the Gentiles, which history vouches for . . . what I am talking about are the phenomena which are quite evidently the result of the force and power of demons: like the story [of] the images of Penates, carried from Troy by Aeneas in his flight."[44] Pagan religion is on the one hand a false social projection, but on the other a very real den of spiritual forces under Rome's foundation.

This demonic spirit of Rome epitomizes the "tragic flaw" in Rome's whole history. For this spirit itself possesses—and entices Romans to be possessed by—the very same qualities Augustine described in his treatment of politics: lust for domination, injustice, greed of glory, craving for praise, deception and coverup. These qualities cohere in this underlying spirit: "We must realize that they are in reality spirits whose only desire is to do harm, who are completely alien from any kind of justice, swollen

---

[43]*COG* 7.27, p. 289.
[44]*COG* 10.16, p. 395

with arrogance, livid with envy, and full of crafty deception."[45] Conflict between Christians and nonbelievers may be inevitable in an epochal challenge, but neither Varro nor any other particular human being represents the real enemy. The true enemy is another. His name is Legion. And the cosmic history of demons that Augustine chronicles reveals the true sin of this enemy: "What other name is there for this fault than pride? 'The beginning of all sin is pride.'"[46]

*The subplot of philosophy.* Augustine begins his foray into Roman philosophy with a historical review, tracing it all the way back to its ancient Greek sources.[47] By now the reader realizes that once again Augustine is seeking to overcome the "extreme incommensurability and untranslatability" that separate the pagan from himself. He is looking for common ground: language and authority that he shares with the challenger. Throughout the book, even in volume 2, he will emphasize the importance of rhetoric that speaks "not merely by appealing to divine authority but also by employing such powers of reason as we can apply for the benefit of unbelievers."[48]

The ground that he finds is none other than the shady groves where Plato and his disciples converse. Romans flock to Plato since "there are thinkers who have rightly recognized Plato's pre-eminence over the pagan philosophers and have won praise for the penetration and accuracy of their judgment, and enjoy a widespread reputation as his followers."[49] Augustine shares a deep and genuine affection for the Greek philosopher and his tradition. Neo-Platonic writers played a key role in Augustine's personal history. In his *Confessions* he recounts how reading them delivered him from his Manichaean beliefs. This deliverance was the immediate prequel to his conversion to Christ, a key syllable that revealed the Word to him.[50]

Augustine saves his treatment of Plato for the end of volume 1 because

[45]*COG* 8.22, p. 329.
[46]*COG* 12.6, p. 477.
[47]*COG* 8.2, p. 299.
[48]*COG* 19.1, p. 843.
[49]*COG* 8.4, p. 304.
[50]See Augustine, *Confessions*, trans. R. S. Pine-Coffin (New York: Penguin, 1987), bks. 5, 7. See also Brown, *Augustine of Hippo* (Berkeley: University of California Press, 1969), pp. 88-100.

Platonic thought constitutes the nearest bridge to the Christian metanarrative that he will begin in volume 2. He maintains a significant tract of common ground with Platonic philosophy, for "we rank such thinkers above all others and acknowledge them as representing the closest approximation to our Christian position."[51] He commends specific Platonic insights such as the understanding that the Supreme Good is God, that human beings need the light of God to see truly, that a philosopher is to love God, and other compatible truths.[52] He even tries to suggest the historical possibility that Plato learned from the Hebrew prophets.[53] He can comfortably call on this shared authority to correct many aspects of the challengers' story, such as the Roman conception of demons as mediators between humankind and God: "We have on our side, in opposition to those practices, the master of their philosophical school, and their great authority, Plato himself."[54]

Plato and his followers, it would seem, are so very close to the Christian story that they can practically reach out and touch the gospel—except for one problem. They refuse to acknowledge some crucial points in the story like the incarnation and the resurrection. It is tragic how close the Platonists are. Only a few corrections would be needed to bring them to the full truth. Some of those reworkings lie so close that a disciple of Plato, Porphyry, "saw what his master failed to see" and perceived that resurrection could conceivably happen.[55] Indeed, Augustine demonstrates that if Plato, Porphyry and other pagan philosophers could submit to each other's correction, they could all be brought to the true faith.[56]

Augustine strikes a clear note of tragedy:

> In spite of your irregular terminology you Platonists have here some kind of an intuition of the goal to which we must strive, however dimly seen through the obscurities of a subtle imagination. And yet you refuse to recognize the incarnation of the unchanging Son of God, which brings us sal-

---

[51]*COG* 8.10, p. 311

[52]*COG* 8.4-10, pp. 304-10.

[53]*COG* 8.11-12, pp. 313-51.

[54]*COG* 8.18, p. 324.

[55]*COG* 10.31, p. 419.

[56]*COG* 22.27, pp. 1079-80.

vation, so that we can arrive at those realities in which we believe, and which we can in some small measure comprehend. Thus you see, to some extent, though from afar off and with clouded vision, the country in which we must find our home; but you do not keep to the road along which we must travel.[57]

The Platonists have come far along the road, but at the last possible juncture they take the wrong fork. Augustine very much wants the Romans themselves to feel this pathos. He conducts an imaginary dialogue with Plato and his pupil Porphyry, hoping that their Roman descendants will overhear and not repeat the tragedy:

> If only you had recognized the grace of God through Jesus Christ our Lord! If only you had been able to see his incarnation, in which he took a human soul and body, as the supreme instance of grace! But what can I do? I know that it is to no avail that I speak to a dead man, to no avail, that is, as far as you are concerned. But there are people who hold you in high regard, who are attached to you by reason of some kind of a love of wisdom, or a superstitious interest in those magic arts which you should never have studied, and they are the audience to whom my colloquy with you is really directed, and it may be that for them it is not in vain.[58]

Yet for all his hope, Augustine knows the real problem runs deeper than mere mistakes in philosophical reasoning. Once again pride rears its head. Augustine unveils it again near the end of volume 1:

> Why is it, then, that when the Christian faith is urged upon you, you straightway forget, or pretend to have no knowledge of, your customary argument and doctrines? What reason is there for your refusal to become Christians on account of opinions which are your own though you yourselves attack them? It can only be that Christ came in humility, and you are proud.[59]

Simply engaging the challengers on their terms will not be enough. The tragic flaw so defines them that they will still dig in their heels with pride: "But humility was the necessary condition for submission to this

---

[57]*COG* 10.29, p. 414.
[58]Ibid.
[59]*COG* 10.29, p. 416.

truth; and it is no easy task to persuade the proud necks of you philosophers to accept this yoke. . . . Now perhaps you are ashamed to have your errors corrected? Here again is a fault which is only found in the proud."[60] They will resist full correction on their own ground.

*Summary.* Augustine responds to his challengers with a willingness to meet on their turf. He inhabits the pagan worldview with appreciation and sympathy. But he also enters in order to retell the pagan story. Using the pagans' own accounts of politics, religion and philosophy, Augustine deconstructs the deconstructionist, unveils the unveiler. In Augustine's rendition, the pagan story is revealed as a tale of human pride. Yet Augustine realizes that such retellings are themselves inadequate to fully convince the pagan. The tragic flaw of pride dominates too much of his challengers' terrain, seizes too much of their heart. Their eyes must be lifted to a new land, their heart captivated by a new tale.

### Capturing Challengers

Volume 2 formally begins Augustine's own metanarrative. Of course he already has begun in many ways. The challengers' subplots have already been reworked to serve as strands in his metanarrative of the "City of God." However, even though the challengers provide elements for Augustine's story, the City of God is decidedly not just an amalgam of Rome's recently reinterpreted subplots. Rather, the City of God story will capture those subplots within a far wider narrative net. And this net will pull everything in its wake toward a fundamentally new conclusion. Thus Augustine's metanarrative is a captivating tale in the truest sense of that term. A narrative captivates audience members when it encompasses their disparate experiences, draws them into a more compelling story and finally brings them to a greater clarity about reality. The tale Augustine tells is far wider, more compelling and more clarifying than any other.

*A wider narrative net.* Augustine's story tells the origins, developments and ends of the two cities, mortal and heavenly. As volume 2 opens he immediately establishes how much wider his story is than the challengers'. His story extends considerably back past Roman history, past

---

[60]*COG* 10.29, pp. 415-16.

human history itself: "The beginning of the two cities had already been seen in the angels."[61] Likewise, he establishes by his narrative that biblical wisdom predates pagan wisdom because Abraham lived long before the Greeks and their philosophy.[62] Finally, he devotes chapter after chapter to the different ancient kingdoms of Israel before finally deigning to bring Rome into the scene, and even then with comparatively fewer lines.[63]

Augustine deliberately tailors his story to evoke the tragic flaw that ran through the pagan story. Both the rebellious angels and the first humans fell into the earthly city because they were "delighted rather with their own power, as though they themselves were their own Good."[64] This pride recurs as the defining distinction between the two cities: "We see then that the two cities were created by two kinds of love: the earthly city was created by self-love reaching the point of contempt for God, the Heavenly City by the love of God carried as far as the contempt of self. In fact, the earthly city glories in itself, the Heavenly City glories in the Lord."[65]

Although Rome plays a relatively small role in this epic, it is not entirely absent. Augustine captures Romans' attention by occasionally bringing familiar characters back onstage. Such appearances frequently feature the underlying flaw shared by the "earthly city" and Rome. For instance, when Augustine recounts the story of the first human brothers, he weaves Cain's murder of Abel with Romulus's murder of Remus, emphasizing that both killed because "anyone whose aim was to glory in the exercise of power would obviously enjoy less power if his sovereignty was diminished by a living partner."[66]

Augustine also features this flaw to explain the challengers' story. He has already unveiled the real nature of Rome in volume 1; now he seeks to interpret for Rome why it possesses (and is possessed by) that demonic nature. For instance, the account of Adam and Eve's fall—an event moti-

---

[61]*COG* 12.1, p. 471.
[62]*COG* 18.37, p. 812.
[63]*COG* 17.23, p. 759.
[64]*COG* 12.1, p. 471.
[65]*COG* 14.28, p. 593.
[66]*COG* 15.5, pp. 600-601.

vated by pride—includes a lengthy discussion about why all people give in
to that sin. He tells his story to emphasize that sin results from will and
choice, and that his explanation is superior to rival stories such as the
Platonic explanation.[67]

Establishing a story's superior explanatory power is crucial in deter-
mining whether it can capture all other challengers. A metanarrative
must not only explain an external reality better than other stories; it must
also explain the other stories themselves.[68] There are analogies of this
process in the history of science. For example, Einstein's theory of general relativity achieved status as the reigning paradigm in astrophysics
partly because it explained the peculiarities of Mercury's orbit much better than the Newtonian account could. But general relativity gained pre-
eminence especially because it could point to exactly where it succeeded
and Newton failed. Einstein put his finger on the one flawed assumption
in Newton—an assumption that only his own model could uncover—and
thereby won the day.[69] In other words, a metanarrative must provide a
metaexplanation: *why* it explains correctly while the other story fails.

Similarly, Augustine is not content merely to reveal the errors in the
pagan stories; he also wants to show that only his story can unmask the
underlying flaw. For instance, he argues that only the humility of Christ
can uncover the blinding spirit of pride in Rome's religion: "This religion, the one true religion, had the power to prove that the gods of the
nations are unclean demons. . . . Man is set free from their monstrous
and blasphemous domination when he believes in him who achieved
his resurrection by the example of a humility as great as the pride

---

[67]*COG* 12.3, p. 473; 12.6-9, pp. 479-83; and especially 14.5, p. 554.

[68]See Alasdair MacIntyre, *Three Rival Versions of Moral Enquiry* (Notre Dame, Ind.: University of Notre Dame Press, 1990), pp. 81, 125.

[69]For this illustration I am indebted to Catherine Crouch, instructor of physics at Harvard
University. Any inaccuracies in or misapplications of the example are strictly mine. As I (a
hopeless nonscientist) understand it, general relativity showed that Newton's assumption
that space and time are unaffected by the presence of objects does not hold across the
board. Thus it failed to account for why Mercury's orbit near the mass of the sun might
alter measurements. For similar examples of how one paradigm comes to supplant another
in science, see Christopher Kaiser, *Creation and the History of Science* (Grand Rapids,
Mich.: Eerdmans, 1991); and Charles Thaxton and Nancy Pearcey, *The Soul of Science*
(Wheaton, Ill.: Crossway, 1994).

which brought about the fall of demons."[70]

Augustine then goes on to explain the failures in Varro's theories: "Varro does his best to explain their ceremonies by supposing a reference to the system of nature, in an effort to lend respectability to obscene activities. But he fails to find a way to square his theory with the facts and give it any consistency."[71] Varro or any pagan can truly understand his own failures only by submitting to the Christian paradigm: "Let him acknowledge the true religion, by which the demons are unmasked and overcome."[72]

One can trace how Augustine repeats this explanatory process with other subplots in the challengers' story, such as why pagan philosophers failed to conceive of a truly universal religion or why Rome could never truly maintain its empire.[73] The important point is that when two stories collide, the decisive battle is over which story will see into the other, which will unveil which. In *City of God* Augustine will make sure he reserves the wider perspective for the biblical metanarrative. All other stories suffer from too limited and cramped a view on reality.

*A more compelling tale.* As Augustine has already noted, prideful Rome will stubbornly resist accepting the biblical story. How then will it be compelled to take its place within this wider metanarrative? Augustine has already exposed the pagan narrative's flaws and explained its failures. One might reasonably expect that at this point he would demand that his challengers abandon their utterly hopeless story.

But Augustine issues no such ultimatum. To "take captive every thought" does not mean to "wipe out every thought." Our Einsteinian analogy illustrates this important distinction. While Einstein's theory clearly proved itself superior to Newtonian physics, general relativity did not totally eradicate the older school. High school students today still

---

[70]*COG* 7.33, p. 294.
[71]Ibid.
[72]*COG* 7.35, p. 297.
[73]See *COG* 10.32, pp. 421, 424, for how Porphyry failed to conceive of a universal religion because of his ignorance of Christianity and his assumption that imperial persecution would wipe it out. See *COG* 19.7, p. 861; and 16.5, p. 658, for how Rome failed to see that it could never unite the Empire under one language because it had no way of knowing that it was simply reenacting the story of Babel and Babylon.

study Newtonian physics. Newtonian physics has been "captured," decisively relativized so that it can no longer claim status as the metaexplanation of reality. But it still retains a place in the table of contents.

In *City of God* Augustine seeks to move pagans by showing them that their story properly belongs at a wider table. Like the master in Jesus' parable of the great banquet, he "compel[s] people to come in" to his metanarrative. He compels by demonstrating that the pagans' deepest hungers, properly understood, can be satisfied only in this wider story.[74] Thus for all his deconstruction of the challenger's story, Augustine does not obliterate it totally. He seeks to redeem it.

An excellent example of Augustine's strategy—and of his consistent and uncanny anticipation of postmodernism—can be found in his discussion of the political subplot of *pax Romana*. Rome hungers for universal peace. In fact, "there is no man who does not wish for peace."[75] Postmodernism has also noted such desires—and sought to obliterate them. One of postmodernism's most dominant themes (and self-contradictions) is its totalizing rejection of "totalizing aims" like universal peace. According to the postmodern story, universal aims invariably lead to the eradication of "the different." Racial, sexual, national and all other types of oppression result when one group claims to possess some "truth for all" like universal peace.[76] Once again we discover that postmoderns simply repeat insights that Augustine had already articulated many centuries ago:

> I shall be told that the Imperial City has been at pains to impose on conquered people not only her yoke but her language also, as a bond of peace and fellowship, so that there should be no lack of interpreters but even a profusion of them. True; but think of the cost of this achievement! Consider the scale of those wars, with all that slaughter of human beings, all the human blood that was shed![77]

From this shared insight, however, Augustine derives a very different

---

[74]The quote is taken from Luke 14:23 NRSV.
[75]*COG* 19.12, p. 866.
[76]See J. Richard Middleton and Brian J. Walsh, *Truth Is Stranger Than It Used to Be* (Downers Grove, Ill.: InterVarsity Press, 1995), pp. 35-36, for an excellent summary of this aspect of postmodernism.
[77]*COG* 19.7, p. 861.

diagnosis. Postmoderns count the terrible cost of the desire for universal peace and conclude that all such desires are false and should be totally renounced. In contrast, for all his deconstruction of pagan Rome, Augustine maintains that its desire for peace is genuine. Indeed, he would reply to the postmodern challenger that to renounce this desire is to obliterate human nature. Augustine insists: "[Human beings] cannot help loving peace of some kind or other. For no creature's perversion is so contrary to nature as to destroy the very last vestiges of its nature."[78] The real problem lies elsewhere. Not surprisingly, Augustine points to the tragic flaw that afflicts not just Rome but all humankind. Pride routinely perverts human methods of attaining peace, as persons seek to satisfy their desire by "imposing their will upon those people's lives" and "impos[ing] on them their own conditions of peace."[79]

Augustine wants Rome to retain its hunger for peace but renounce the way its tragic will to power perverts that desire. Significantly, in the middle of his analysis of *pax Romana* he suddenly launches into a theological/philosophical discourse on the nature of evil. In a passage that appears seemingly out of the blue, he goes to great lengths to deny an ultimate ontology to evil. In fact, Augustine insists that "not even the nature of the Devil himself is evil, in so far as it is a nature; it is perversion that makes it evil. . . . God, in punishing, does not chastise the good which he created, but the evil which the Devil has committed."[80]

On the surface this seems like one of the many digressions in *City of God* which lead scholars like John O'Meara to eschew seeking a deeper unity within the work: "with each book the topics are so disparate as to defy broad analysis."[81] But seen in the light of the strategy of "taking every thought captive," this passage represents Augustine's eagerness to take his captive alive. Contra Nietzsche, Augustine does not accord evil an ultimate ontology; he refuses to accept that violence and death are intrinsic to human life and desires. So whereas postmodernism's remedy tends to suffocate universal human desires, Augustine seeks to breathe more life into them.

---

[78]*COG* 19.12, p. 869.
[79]*COG* 19.12, p. 867.
[80]*COG* 19.13, p. 871.
[81]O'Meara, introduction to *COG*, p. xxxvi

Augustine always seeks to encourage signs of true life in his opponents. In a sermon describing a different conflict, one with Pelagian heretics, he proclaims:

> Give me a man in love: he knows what I mean. Give me one who yearns; give me one who is hungry; give me one far away in this desert, who is thirsty and sighs for the spring of the Eternal country. Give me that sort of man: he knows what I mean. But if I speak to a cold man, he just does not know what I am talking about.[82]

Only a passionately living opponent can be moved by the gospel metanarrative, the story of a true passion and life.

Augustine is also eager to take his captive in peace. As John Milbank has persuasively demonstrated, postmodernism must give violence a prior ontology, which makes it impossible for postmodern thinkers to conceive of a nontotalizing, true peace.[83] Augustine confidently tells a story that climaxes in real, abiding peace. But unlike the many false and indeed bloody promises of peace that have been made by human rulers (and by religious leaders and parties) in history, this peace is not found in the storyteller's own plans. In a massive work titled *City of God*, one would expect the author to give in to the temptation to insert at least some of his own political agendas, much the way Plato did in *The Republic*. But this book continues to baffle scholars who try to read it as a political text, because Augustine's story contains no economic theories or social reforms promising to achieve lasting peace. Augustine is all too aware of the dangers inherent in the perverted desire to impose one's own conditions of peace. So his tale of peace points far beyond himself.

This peace lies in the future consummation of the City of God. The earthly city's stories, schemes and plots to secure lasting peace are hopeless: "What shall we say of the city? The larger the city, the more is its forum filled with civil lawsuits and criminal trials, even if that city be at peace, free from the alarms or—what is more frequent—the bloodshed of

---

[82]Quoted in Brown, *Augustine of Hippo*, p. 375.
[83]John Milbank, *Theology and Social Theory: Beyond Secular Reason* (Oxford: Blackwell, 1990), pp. 278-325. In his conclusion Milbank similarly argues that Augustine's *City of God* provides Christians with an alternative ontology.

sedition and civil war. It is true that cities are at times exempt from those occurrences; they are never free from the danger of them."[84] But only when humans enter the great story of God will they satisfy their desire for true peace. Indeed, a completed relationship with God is peace itself. This peace relativizes all other claims to peace: "And so long as he is in this mortal body, he is a pilgrim in a foreign land, away from God; therefore he walks by faith, not by sight. That is why he views all peace, of body or of soul, or of both, *in relation to that peace which exists between mortal man and immortal God.*"[85]

Hope is critical for the one walking as a "pilgrim in a foreign land" because this peace will be fully unveiled only near the end of the path. When the final judgment occurs, the City of God will emerge completely out of the violent shadows of the earthly city. Then and only then "there will be true peace, where none will suffer attack from within himself nor from any foe outside. . . . There that precept will find fulfillment: 'Be still, and know that I am God.' That will truly be the greatest of Sabbaths; a Sabbath that has no evening, the Sabbath that the Lord approved at the beginning of creation."[86]

To take captive the challengers' story alive, in peace and especially with hope—this is the end of Augustine's rhetorical strategy. Conflict may be the unavoidable starting point and inevitable context, but this strategy points to a genuine resolution.

Augustine repeatedly attempts to captivate his challengers in this manner. He encourages pagans' heartfelt desire to know the source of life, but they need to look to the Creator—not the created—to satisfy that aim.[87] He praises the Romans' eagerness for "friendship" and "mediation" with the supernatural, only hoping they will realize that true peace can come only with the Mediator Jesus.[88] And he appeals to the philosophers' longing for the Eternal Good in order to entice them to hope in the eternal City of God.[89]

---

[84]See *COG* 19.5, p. 859; 19.27-28, pp. 892-94.
[85]*COG* 19.14, p. 873, emphasis mine.
[86]*COG* 22.30, pp. 1088, 1090.
[87]*COG* 7.29-30, p. 291.
[88]See *COG* 9.15, p. 359; 19.9, p. 864.
[89]*COG* 8.1, p. 298; 19.4, p. 852.

*A new clarity. City of God* concludes with the final judgment and the
peace that this final act unfurls. The whole narrative flow sweeps toward
this final unveiling. "For everything that is here said about those human
beings who are not citizens of that City is said with this purpose," Augustine reminds the reader "that the City may show up to advantage, may be
thrown into relief, by contrast with its opposite."[90]

In the final judgment, all is unveiled because God himself is unveiled.
This self-disclosure brings ultimate clarity about all reality:

> For such reasons it is possible, it is indeed most probable, that we shall
> then see the physical bodies of the new heaven and the new earth in such a
> fashion as to observe God in utter clarity and distinctness, seeing him
> present everywhere and governing the whole material scheme of things . . .
> It will not be as it is now, when the invisible realities of God are appre-
> hended and observed through the material things of his creation, and are
> partially apprehended by means of a puzzling reflection in a mirror.[91]

In the light of this final judgment, all of history's ambiguities are
finally resolved. God himself draws the narrative to its natural resting
place. Evoking Jesus' parable of the kingdom of God as a fishing net,
Augustine declares: "Both [city of man and City of God] sorts are collected as it were in the dragnet of the gospel, and in this world, as in a sea,
both kinds swim without separation, enclosed in nets until the shore is
reached. There the evil are to be divided from the good."[92] In this narrative net all human stories are captured and clarified for all eternity.

Lest the visible church and individual Christians assume that this ending means their side wins and everyone else loses, Augustine reminds the
reader that the new epistemological clarity will bring surprises. Some who
seemed to walk outside the visible church on earth will end up revealed
as true members of the City of God; other individuals who seemed to
travel "mingled in the Church" will end up revealed as "reprobate"
members of the city of men.[93] In this final chapter we will see that God's

---

[90]*COG* 16.2, pp. 652-53.
[91]*COG* 22.29, p. 1086.
[92]*COG* 18.49, p. 831. See Matthew 13:47-51.
[93]*COG* 18.47, p. 829; 18.49, p. 831.

metanarrative is so wide that he outflanks all the "sides" we may have smugly established in our human conflicts. A wise word to all Christians involved in partisan politics.

One thing is certain about the final act, though: this final unveiling decisively resolves the tragic flaw of the challengers' story. While those who have looked forward in humble faith to this final act will meet God, those who have attempted "to fabricate for themselves an utterly delusive happiness by means of a virtue whose falsity is in proportion to its arrogance" will be destroyed.[94] When God is unveiled fully, the love of God must swallow up the love of self. Pride has no place at the end of all epochs.

For his own epoch Augustine's conclusion opened up a new option of response to the epochal challenge. For Christians of his day the two options of response most often chosen were "withdrawing from the different" and "defending the same." In the former, many Christians so feared the pagan challenge that they sought to remain uncontaminated by any trace of its different learning, much as fundamentalists respond today to postmodern culture (and to any other taint of the "different"). Entire Christian communities such as the Donatists would wall themselves off from any contact with Roman power or culture.[95] However, in *City of God* Augustine showed Christians that they had no need to fear challengers or their learning. The Christian story, especially in its conclusion, could disarm and capture all comers.

Other Christians took the option of defending the same old story of the Eternal City. They continued to believe the Eternal City marriage would triumphantly obliterate the pagan story, even after 410. A prime example of this option is Orosius's *History Versus the Pagans*. In 416 Augustine had commissioned Orosius, a refugee from the collapsed Roman frontier in Spain who was under his patronage, to write a historical apologetic regarding the fall of Rome.[96] Augustine must have shaken his head the following year when he read the resulting manuscript. In *History Versus the Pagans* Orosius simply tried to palliate the barbarian

---

[94]*COG* 19.4, p. 857.
[95]Brown, *Augustine of Hippo*, p. 265.
[96]Robert Markus, *Saeculum* (London: Cambridge University Press, 1970), p. 4.

invasions and reassert the special providential role of Empire.[97]

It is a good guess that Orosius's effort to defend the inherited story redoubled Augustine's sense of urgency in writing his own story. In *City of God* Augustine never defends the inherited narrative of Constantine, Eusebius and Theodosius.[98] Instead, in responding to challengers he also rewrites the narrative lines of the church. Rome is only a bit player in the grand sweep of the church's story. Rome is not the church's savior or marriage partner; only Christ can play those roles. The ultimate celebration of history takes place not at some past coronation of a Roman emperor but at the future wedding feast of the Lamb.

Augustine snaps Christians back to a clarity about their own future. He calls Christians to "renounce the audacious presumption" that they will never face state persecution again.[99] If the church trusts in the human city which claims that all roads lead to itself, then the church will take the wrong fork; it will miss the true "royal road, which alone leads to that kingdom whose glory is not the tottering grandeur of the temporal, but the secure stability of the eternal."[100] As a pastor, Augustine reminds Christians to refrain from needless anxiety over the sack of Rome. The Roman epoch may continue awhile longer, or it may end soon—"who knows what is God's will in this matter?"[101] Either way, the story of the City of God will roll on like a majestic carriage bypassing such historical deadends and detours. Peter Brown pays the aging bishop an apt compliment when he notes: "It is a rare thing to come across a man of sixty, living on the threshold of a great change, who had already come to regard a unique culture and a unique political institution as replaceable, in theory at least."[102]

---

[97]Brown, *Augustine of Hippo*, pp. 295-96.

[98]For an interesting comparison between Augustine's treatment of Constantine and Theodosius, see *COG* 5.19, pp. 212-13, and Markus, *Saeculum*, p. 49. Markus notes that Augustine uses some of the same passages that Eusebius uses, but interprets them very differently, stripping the emperors of any messianic pretensions. See also *COG* 22.6, pp. 1029-1032, for Augustine's final recension of his story compared to Eusebius's recension of his story (discussed in chapter two above).

[99]*COG* 18.52, p. 837.

[100]*COG* 10.32, p. 420.

[101]*COG* 4.7, p. 143. For other Christian writers of Augustine's day who viewed the coming epochs with anxiety about impeding doom, see Markus, *Saeculum*, pp. 25-26.

[102]Brown, *Augustine of Hippo*, p. 266.

It is apt that Augustine draws his massive epic to an end with an implicit bit of advice to Christians in all future epochs. In his final paragraphs he reminds us that in the only story that really matters there are only seven chapters, akin to the seven days of God's creation. These seven chapters are not defined by passing human empires but by the seminal events of the biblical narrative. "If the epochs of history are reckoned as 'days' following the apparent temporal scheme of Scripture," Augustine reasons, then "the coming of Christ in the flesh" represents the beginning of the sixth epoch. "We are now," Augustine declares, "in the sixth epoch." All historical periods that follow Christ's coming—whether the late Roman Empire, Western Christendom or a post-Christian society—are crammed into those few blank pages before the seventh and final chapter of God's judgment and ultimate peace.[103] The self-importance of any period disappears in the joyful anticipation of that last epoch.

Augustine himself could barely contain that joy. All the seemingly irresolvable conflicts he faced faded when he looked forward to the conclusion of all history. On the same year that he began to write *City of God*, he preached a sermon that revealed the hopeful anticipation that kept him going even when his society seemed to be fragmenting:

> When, therefore, death shall be swallowed up in victory, these things will not be there, and there shall be peace—peace full and eternal. We shall be in a kind of city. Brethren, when I speak of that City, and especially when scandals grow great here, I just cannot bring myself to stop.[104]

---

[103]*COG* 23.30, p. 1091. See also 12.13, p. 486, where Augustine describes all historical periods as drops in an ocean.

[104]Quoted in Brown, *Augustine of Hippo*, p. 312.

# 4

# Engaging Religious Pluralism

## SUMMA CONTRA GENTILES

A READER WHO JUMPS STRAIGHT from *City of God* to *Summa contra Gentiles* (hereafter *SCG*) experiences a certain degree of intellectual motion sickness. Gone are references to Roman history and the grand sweep of biblical events; in their place are Aristotelian philosophical terms and a complex flow of rational arguments. However, as seen in chapter two, the two works were composed in corresponding situations. The *SCG* was written by Thomas Aquinas in response to the epochal challenge of Islam, especially in the Falasifa's appropriation of Aristotle. The challengers' philosophical story threatened the Only City story of knowledge. Aristotle, as presented by his Islamic commentators, laid out a path of knowledge that ran outside Christian civilization and learning. Moreover, the challengers' story presented disturbing characterizations of God and humanity.

The *SCG* responds to the epochal challenge with the same underlying strategy found in *City of God*. Aquinas too enters, retells and then ultimately captures his challenger's story. This strategy will dictate my analysis of his work. In many ways the *SCG* is an even more elaborately woven epic than *City of God*; hence my close reading of the text will necessarily focus on a few representative strands. But first it will be helpful to get an overview of the *SCG*'s structure, genre and central dramatic action.

## Structure

Describing the structure of the *SCG* with literary categories like plot and characters will undoubtedly seem jarring to scholars and students reared on conventional philosophical approaches to Aquinas. Faced with a seemingly dense wall of abstraction, the postmodern emphasis on narrative has hardly penetrated the field of Aquinas studies. And indeed one would be short-sighted to impose narrative categories on Aquinas's work simply because they are trendy in the postmodern milieu.

Yet there are some good reasons to at least try on a narrative lens when reading Aquinas in general and the *SCG* in particular. First, Alasdair MacIntyre has argued persuasively that every philosophy is embedded in some "storied tradition"; and he has done so especially while concentrating on Thomism. We cannot escape stories, even if those stories take on the philosophical genre. Second, like any medieval scholar, Thomas Aquinas steeped himself in the biblical worldview, which he understood as being bound to a historical narrative, "per modum narrationis historicae."[1] Studies of his era's preaching (including Aquinas's own sermons), liturgy and church art suggest that this epoch naturally thought in terms of drama.[2]

Third, some recent scholarship has begun to fruitfully point out the narrative structure of the *SCG* in particular.[3] I believe the *SCG* will serve

---

[1]See John Finnis, *Aquinas* (Oxford: Oxford University Press, 1998), p. 54 n.

[2]On the narrative framework of medieval preaching and liturgy, see Hughes Oliphant Old, *The Reading and Preaching of the Scriptures in the Worship of the Christian Church*, vol. 3, *The Medieval Church* (Grand Rapids, Mich.: Eerdmans, 1999), pp. 147-62, 191. See especially pp. 417-30 for how Aquinas himself regularly preached on the key events of the gospel narratives. For Aquinas's commentary on novelists, playwrights, actors and others working in the dramatic arts, see Finnis, *Aquinas*, p. 155 n. For more on the dramatic emphasis of the church in this period, see David Bevington's classic work *Medieval Drama* (Boston: Houghton Mifflin, 1975), especially pp. 1-8. On the narrative dimensions of medieval art see Margaret Miles, *Image as Insight: Visual Understanding in Western Christianity and Secular Culture* (Boston: Beacon, 1985), pp. 71-74.

[3]For example, see Thomas Hibbs, *Dialectic and Narrative in Aquinas: An Interpretation of the "Summa contra Gentiles"* (Notre Dame, Ind.: University of Notre Dame Press, 1995), esp. pp. 2-9. I disagree with much of Hibbs's reading and key assumptions of the *SCG* (as the appendix makes clear), but I do appreciate his general attempt to try on a narrative lens in reading this work.

as a key opening for exploring the narrative dimensions of Aquinas. Thomistic studies have tended to be overdominated by the *Summa Theologica*, which as an encyclopedic summary of topics seems especially removed from narrative. But the *SCG* has long struck scholars as very different from the *Summa Theologica;* in attempts to articulate this distinction, terms like *creative* and *personal* have been used.[4] I propose that narrative terms may further aid the reader seeking to grasp this unique work.

The reader need not accept from the outset that the *SCG* has a narrative structure. The ultimate (although not sole) test of any literary framework ultimately rests in exegesis. The question is whether narrative categories significantly aid the reading of the text. I simply ask the reader (and especially students and scholars of Aquinas) to be open to the possibility and see whether my reading leads to a more coherent understanding of the work as a whole.

There is one final reason to suspect that Aquinas could be read using narrative categories. MacIntyre has argued that Aquinas looked to Augustine as one of his most formative and treasured authorities, that in fact Aquinas saw his task as trying to respond to the Aristotelian challenge without losing his Augustinianism.[5] Thus it would make sense that *City of God*, with its reliance on narrative to respond to an earlier epochal challenge, would inform Aquinas especially as he engaged with his own epochal challenge. And indeed, references to *City of God* are numerous throughout the *SCG*. On occasion Aquinas links the "error of the Saracens" to other errors that Augustine had combated in *City of God*.[6]

More significant than individual citations, however, is the way Aquinas follows the basic structure of *City of God*. Like Augustine, Aquinas organizes his work based on the distinction between the challengers' narrative

---

[4]Ibid., p. 2.

[5]Alasdair MacIntyre, *Three Rival Versions of Moral Enquiry* (Notre Dame, Ind.: University of Notre Dame Press, 1990), pp. 105-26.

[6]See, for example, *SCG* 4.83, p. 316. For more general references to *City of God*, see *SCG* 1.43.14, p. 168; *SCG* 3.10.7, p. 57 (part 1); *SCG* 3.27.11, p. 113 (part 1); *SCG* 3.84.9, p. 16 (part 2); *SCG* 3.93.6, p. 50 (part 2); *SCG* 3.104.12, p. 93 (part 2); *SCG* 3.106.8, p. 99 (part 2); *SCG* 3.107.13, p. 103 (part 2); *SCG* 3.109.2, p. 108 (part 2); *SCG* 3.120.2, p. 134 (part 2); *SCG* 3.128.3, p. 160 (part 2); *SCG* 4.82.11, p. 311.

and the gospel metanarrative. Early in book 1 he introduces this distinction:

> Now to make the first kind of divine truth known, we must proceed through demonstrative arguments, by which our adversary may become convinced. However, since such arguments are not available for the second kind of divine truth, our intention should not be to convince our adversary by arguments. . . . The sole way to overcome an adversary of divine truth is from the authority of Scripture.[7]

In other words, challengers will accept certain terms and authorities; using them, Aquinas can make demonstrative arguments that can convince the challengers of this first kind of divine truth. However, there is a second kind of divine truth which must involve terms and authority from the different story of the Scripture. Challengers will not become convinced by this story immediately; rather they must be overcome by it. In the same chapter Aquinas declares, "One kind of divine truth the investigation of the reason is competent to reach, whereas the other surpasses every effort of the reason."[8] The common story that Aquinas can enter and retell is composed of reason and rational philosophers like Aristotle, but his own metanarrative rests on higher ground.

This distinction between the challengers' story and the gospel metanarrative clearly dictates the overall structure of the work. Aquinas organized the SCG into four books: book 1 deals with the character of God, book 2 with the character of creation and especially human beings, book 3 with providence (how God and creation interact), and book 4 with salvation. In the first three books Aquinas operates very much within the challengers' story while in the fourth book he clearly switches into his own. Anton Pegis comments on this shift: "The exposition of the truths that faith professes and reason investigates occupies St. Thomas during the first three books of the SCG. With the opening of Book IV, he takes up the second part of the exposition of the truth revealed by God, namely the truth that surpasses reason."[9]

---

[7]SCG 1.9.2, p. 77.
[8]SCG 1.9.1, p. 77.
[9]Pegis, introduction to SCG 1, p. 32

The structural distinction between the two stories is further reinforced by the abrupt shift in source material between books 1-3 and book 4. The overwhelming bulk of citations in books 1-3 derive from a wide range of Aristotle's own works and those of his Islamic commentators. Aquinas indwells and reinterprets this vast area of the challengers' story. The Scripture that is used is cited only at the very end of each chapter, after the "demonstrative argument" has already been made. Near the end of book 3, however, a clear transition takes place. The translator of the standard edition of book 3 notes: "The use of Scripture grows quantitatively, and in importance, as the Book progresses. Towards the end, the reader is almost prepared for the shift to the more definitely Scriptural argument of Book Four."[10] Book 4 is dominated by biblical material, with only a few references to Aristotle interspersed. As volume 2 did in *City of God*, book 4 weaves the reworked Aristotelian story into a larger tale.

The structure of the "plot" of *SCG* is fairly straightforward. In books 1-2 the main characters are introduced and their main traits and motivations developed. Aquinas focuses on God and humankind as his main actors, an unsurprising choice given that the epochal challenge presented disquieting portrayals of those two characters. Book 3 features the tragic crisis: human reason suffers unfortunate limits in its ability to know God. Like any good storyteller, Aquinas has foreshadowed this crisis early in book 1:

> Hence, if the human intellect comprehends the substance of some thing, for example, that of a stone or of a triangle, no intelligible characteristic belonging to that thing surpasses the grasp of the human reason. But this does not happen to us in the case of God. For the human intellect is not able to reach a comprehension of the divine substance through its natural power.[11]

Then in the first half of book 4 God steps back to the fore as the key actor. Book 4's lengthy treatment of the incarnation represents the plot's climax, resolving the tragic tension in the challenger's story. Finally, the

---

[10]Vernon J. Bourke, introduction to *Summa contra Gentiles*, bk. 3, trans. Vernon J. Bourke (Notre Dame, Ind.: University of Notre Dame Press, 1975), p. 15.
[11]*SCG* 1.3.3, pp. 63-64.

second half of book 4 presents the concluding scene of the beatitude where humankind eternally experiences God.

## Genre

Most readers miss the narrative structure of the *SCG* because of its philosophical genre.[12] The work is so philosophical and abstract that it only occasionally mentions Islamic history and religious doctrine. This has caused some scholars to object to Ramon of Penyaforte's correspondence with Aquinas as the historical occasion for *SCG*. Indeed, on the surface the work hardly seems like an evangelism textbook for Dominican missionaries. I have devoted an entire appendix to this issue. For now, however, it is worth noting Pegis's response to such objections:

> There are no serious historical reasons for refusing to accept this testimony [about Ramon's letter]. The objection that the SCG is too intellectual in character to be a manual of apologetics for missionaries is not a very strong one. St. Thomas himself may very well have thought that the SCG was precisely the sort of work needed by Christian missionaries in Spain face to face with the high intellectual culture of the Moslem world. Seen from this point of view, the SCG is a manual of apologetics against the intellectual picture of the universe created for the Western world by the translation of the writings of Aristotle and his followers into Latin in the course of the 12th and 13th centuries. This is a perfectly understandable objective. In a large sense, therefore, the SCG is part of the Christian intellectual reaction against Arabian intellectual culture, and especially against Arabian Aristotelianism. To the Arabs, and especially to Averroës, Aristotle was philosophy.[13]

It is important to reiterate Pegis's point that there are no serious historical reasons to reject the missiological context of *SCG*. Scholars who do reject such a context refer not to any extratextual evidence but to the genre and structure of the text. In the pages that follow I hope it will be

---

[12]For another interesting although somewhat different interpretation of the narrative structure of *SCG*, see Hibbs, *Dialectic and Narrative*, pp. 7-8.

[13]Pegis, introduction to *SCG* 1, p. 21. For another influential commentator on Aquinas who shares this basic assessment, see Anthony Kenny, *Aquinas on Mind* (London: Routledge, 1993), p. 13.

evident that the genre and structure actually show that Aquinas's intentions in *SCG* were the same as Augustine's in *City of God:* both take the occasion of a specific request from an evangelist to respond to the broader epochal challenge facing all evangelists of their day.

*SCG* certainly is a very complex work, filled with elaborate concepts like "quiddity" and "ratiocinative reasoning." Yet at the same time it is a work stripped to the bare essentials of philosophy. The *SCG* asks how one knows truth, how an "intellect comprehends the substance of some thing."[14] The epochal challenge centered on the very nature of knowledge, especially the knowledge of God. Islam had invaded the epoch on this philosophical front; Aquinas must respond on that front if there is to be any place of encounter other than the bloody battlefield. Islam had issued a challenge in the language of Aristotle; Aquinas must respond in the same language if he is to converse and not crusade.

Aquinas especially recognized that his fellow Dominicans needed a more effective rhetorical strategy than what had previously been attempted. Most Christians who eschewed the military crusades and sought to preach to the Islamic world still waged the intellectual equivalent of the crusades. Their preaching was done in the polemic style, which involved criticizing Muslim doctrine revealed in the Qur'an on the basis of its violation of Christian doctrine revealed in the Bible.[15] Obviously neither accepted the other's terms or authorities. Without any common ground, Christians could hope only to outshout their opponents. Muslims had little reason to accept this sort of preaching, and felt they had plenty of reason to execute those who so hectored them.

The way both sides resorted to rhetorical or physical violence was repugnant to a philosopher like Thomas. This is why in the only section of *SCG* that can be even remotely construed as a polemic against Islam, Aquinas's real argument is that in Islam's rapid expansion it had not relied on truly compelling rhetoric. Islam historically grew in numbers, Aquinas notes (rather accurately), because "Mohammed forced others to become his follow-

---

[14]*SCG* 1.3.3, p. 63.

[15]For a detailed discussion of this subject, see the classic work by Norman Daniel, *Islam and the West* (Edinburgh: Edinburgh University Press, 1960).

ers by the violence of his arms."[16] Indeed, in our age where the Christian crusades are so widely (and rightly) castigated, it is forgotten that Islamic
crusades had even more completely obliterated native cultures and narratives, the effects of which are still felt in those conquered lands.[17]

Regardless of who has committed more violence, Aquinas strongly
warns Christians against the intellectual and cultural versions of the crusades. He warns evangelists to refrain from polemics, "for the very inadequacy of the arguments would rather strengthen them [the unbelievers]
in their error, since they would imagine that our acceptance of the truth
of faith was based on such weak arguments."[18] Polemicists end up portraying Christianity as irrational, subjective and incomprehensible to the
nonbeliever, in much the way that some of today's Christians, not knowing how else to articulate reasons for their faith, end up mumbling about
some vague leap in the dark.

Thomas insists that we must begin with a common language. The
Christian cannot ask the Islamic challengers to immediately leap across
into the biblical metanarrative:

> The Mohammedans and the pagans do not agree with us in accepting the
> authority of any Scripture, by which they may be convinced of their error.
> Thus, against the Jews we are able to argue by means of the Old Testament,
> while against heretics we are able to argue by means of the New Testament.
> But the Mohammedans and the pagans accept neither the one nor the other.

"We must, therefore," Aquinas concludes, "have recourse to the natural
reason, to which all men are forced to give their assent."[19] His eagerness to
engage with Muslims on the basis of a common natural reason led Norman
Daniel, the eminent twentieth-century historian of Christian-Islamic relations, to give Aquinas the title "the great but lonely exception."[20]

---

[16]*SCG* 1.6.4, p. 73.
[17]For an excellent description of the contemporary effects of the Islamic crusade, see V. S
Naipaul's *Beyond Belief: Islamic Excursions Among the Converted People* (New York: Ran
dom House, 1998).
[18]*SCG* 1.9.2, pp. 77-78.
[19]*SCG* 1.2.3, p. 62.
[20]Quoted in James Waltz, "Muhammad and the Muslims in St. Thomas Aquinas," *The Mus
lim World* 66 (April 1976): 90.

Shaping the philosophical genre was also crucial to Aquinas because of how the epochal challenge was already affecting contemporary Christian philosophers. Often the most significant and lasting damage done by an epochal challenger lies not in the actual challenge itself but in the misshapen Christian response to the challenge. For instance, Michael Buckley has shown how sixteenth-century Christian philosophical attempts to respond to skeptics actually gave birth to the intellectual character of modern atheism. Moreover, those philosophical adaptations left modern Christianity particularly vulnerable to the arguments of subsequent generations of atheists.[21]

Aquinas could already see the dangers of misshapen philosophical responses. One of the leading centers of Christian philosophy in his day was the University of Paris. Aquinas himself spent two lengthy stints studying at Paris, received his license to teach from the university, and later taught there for several years. The University of Paris was organized into the Faculty of Theology (where Aquinas taught) and the Faculty of Arts (consisting of science, the humanities and philosophy). As early as the beginning of the thirteenth century, the Faculty of Arts had sought to teach on Averroës, Avicenna and other Islamic commentators of Aristotle just becoming known in the West. The local synod, most likely supported by the Faculty of Theology, banned the practice.[22]

By 1255, however, a group of young enthusiasts called the Latin Averroists successfully petitioned to have the university reinstate the reading of Aristotelian works. The Latin Averroists, based in the Faculty of Arts, quickly sought to create a place for Aristotle that would be secure from the theological interference experienced in the past. By 1260, one of the leading proponents of Latin Averrroism, Siger of Brabant, was proposing to split off the teaching of the Faculty of Arts from that of the Faculty of Theology. He argued that Aristotle demonstrated the autonomy of phi-

---

[21]Michael J. Buckley, *At the Origins of Modern Atheism* (New Haven, Conn.: Yale University Press, 1987).

[22]Unless otherwise noted, the following description of the "war of the faculties" at Paris is taken from Jan A. Aertsen, "Aquinas's Philosophy in Its Historical Setting," in *The Cambridge Companion to Aquinas*, ed. Norman Kretzmann and Eleonore Stump (Cambridge: Cambridge University Press, 1993), pp. 20-25.

losophy and natural reason from theology. Philosophical reason produced truths in one independent realm, while faith produced truths in another independent realm. The two realms were separate and "incommensurable"; they could be—indeed should be—separated from one another. Siger stated the case for this intellectual trench so forcefully that later readers have even interpreted him to mean that what could be true in one realm could actually be false in the other.[23]

*SCG* was sandwiched between Aquinas's direct experiences with the Latin Averroist movement. Before beginning the *SCG*, Aquinas had studied and taught in the Faculty of Theology from 1252 to 1259 when the movement was emerging. After completing *SCG* at the University of Naples (1259-1265), he returned in 1269 to teach theology at Paris once again.[24] While the Latin Averroists were not the main target of *SCG*, their vision haunted Aquinas. After returning to Paris, he devoted himself to countering the separation that Siger and his movement were proposing. He wrote tract after tract against Siger, seeking to preserve the unity of knowledge in the university. Chesterton vividly describes (as only Chesterton can) the tone of these tracts:

> It is extraordinarily interesting to note that this is the one occasion when the Dumb Ox really came out like a wild bull. When he stood up to answer Siger of Brabant, he was altogether transfigured, and the very style of his sentences, which is a thing like the tone of a man's voice, is suddenly altered. . . . There is a ring in the words altogether beyond the almost impersonal patience he maintained in debate with so many enemies.[25]

Aquinas argued so passionately because he detected higher stakes than administrative arrangements between two academic departments. In

---

[23]See MacIntyre, *Three Rival Versions of Moral Enquiry*, p. 123. This was the dominant interpretation of Siger of Brabant for decades, but most modern scholars now do not believe he was actually proposing the "two truths" theory.

[24]One must note again that the precise dating of Aquinas's movements and writings is a difficult and debated exercise. This particular account draws from Finnis, *Aquinas*, pp. 8-9; Norman Kretzmann, "Thomas Aquinas," in *Routledge Encyclopedia of Philosophy* (London: Routledge, 1998), 1:329; and Ralph McInerny, *St. Thomas Aquinas* (Boston: Twayne, 1977), p. 11.

[25]G. K. Chesterton, *Saint Thomas Aquinas: The Dumb Ox* (New York: Doubleday, 1956), p. 94.

*Summa contra Gentiles* he had discerned the profound dangers of permitting an epistemological trench between faith and reason. Such a trench would inevitably widen into all sorts of disastrous divisions for Christianity. First of all, as mentioned, Christians could not hope to lead Muslims to the higher land of faith if the common bridge of reason were destroyed. Second, the Christian mind would be consigned to a sort of intellectual schizophrenia, jumping back and forth between faith and reason, and bearing any contradictions with a fatalistic shrug: "So what?" Such contradictions would inevitably break down the unity of truth, for "it is therefore impossible that what belongs to philosophy be contrary to what belongs to faith."[26] Finally and most important, the God of Christianity would become divided. All truth flowed from "God Himself, Who is truth one and simple"; a split in truth would wind its unavoidable way back to the source.[27] God is One: the God of theology must be the same God of philosophy.

By definition, an epochal challenge involves enormous division and conflict. For those who seek to respond to the challenge, it is terribly tempting to give in to the spirit of the age. If you wish to stand in this age, this spirit whispers, you must stand on one side or the other: you must defend the old epoch as a crusader or appease the new challenger as an Latin Averroist; you must accept theology or practice science; you must believe or reason.

*SCG* is difficult to read because it was written by a man caught in a difficult age. The intensely philosophical genre of the book testifies to Aquinas's desire to participate in his age without falling captive to its divisive spirit. Aquinas must laboriously connect with his challengers without lazily conceding; he must point out important distinctions while protecting against irreconcilable divisions. He must painstakingly fashion a way out of the impasse that is the epoch. Philosophy gives him the necessary tools to do so, and in *Summa contra Gentiles* we witness a master craftsman at work.

### Central Dramatic Action

This work animates the central dramatic action of *SCG*, which may be

---

[26]Quoted in Pegis, introduction to *SCG* 1, p. 25.
[27]*SCG* 1.9.1, p. 77.

summed up in the word *reunite*. Throughout the book Aquinas seeks to
reunite one potentially fractured pairing after another. He reconnects
faith and reason, philosophy and theology, Aristotle and Christian doctrine, soul and body, head and heart, intellect and senses, knowledge and
experience, thought and being. All of these topics are discussed at length
in *SCG*. In every case, Aquinas seeks to reunite them in an organic and
well-defined relationship.[28]

The act of reuniting propels Aquinas's epistemological story. Progress
from being one who does not know to becoming one who does know
comes only by participating in a story that actually resolves these tensions. Our epoch demonstrates the consequences of seeking to tell a story
of knowledge that avoids—rather than truly resolves—tension. Like Siger
of Brabant, the Enlightenment sought to alleviate any hint of epistemological tension by splitting the unities *SCG* seeks to preserve. Descartes
responded to his existential doubt by avoiding experiential knowledge
altogether, introducing a radical cleavage between thought and experience. The rest of modernity followed him in sundering the union of mind
and body, head and heart, and other related pairings. Postmodern
descendants of this modern project thus have inherited a self so radically
fractured that the postmodern self feels practically incapable of knowing
anything fully. With so many seemingly unresolvable contradictions
already multiplying in one's own self, it is no wonder that postmoderns
like Alex (the student described in chapter one) remain unaffected by yet
another contradiction thrust upon them by an apologist. "So what?" Alex
shrugged; he might as well have said, "So what else is new?"

Immobilized by radical doubt, this rent self is also rendered incapable
of sustained action in any direction. Charles Taylor, in his landmark study
*Sources of the Self: The Making of the Modern Identity*, noted that psy-
chopathologists have witnessed a sea change in the "presenting symptoms" of patients: whereas earlier generations complained of "specific
phobias and fixations" that prevented them from attaining well-delin-

---

[28]For instance, see *SCG* 1.9.1-4, p. 77-78, on how faith and reason relate; *Summa contra
Gentiles*, bk. 2, trans. with introduction by James F. Anderson (Notre Dame, Ind.: University of Notre Dame Press, 1975), pt. 70, sec. 1-3, pp. 210-11, on how the intellect is united
with the senses; *SCG* 2.71.1-3, pp. 212-13, on how the soul is united with the body.

eated goals, recent patients arrive with "main complaints [that] centre around 'ego loss,' or a sense of emptiness, flatness, futility, lack of purpose, or loss of self-esteem."[29] Those of us who minister to this generation daily encounter firsthand the paralyzed nature of what some observers call the "decentered self or the "depleted self."[30] The life stories of these doubting selves seem to have ground to a halt.

In contrast, Aquinas's story of knowledge is filled with vigorous movement, action and drama. Like Homer's *Odyssey* or Jesus' parable of the prodigal son, Aquinas's tale is of homecoming, only on a grand philosophical scale. The central dramatic action in *SCG* is the epic reunion of humanity with God. This central dramatic action of "reunite" explains the order of the four books in *SCG*. The epic begins with book 1, titled "God," the home to "all blessedness" who existed before time.[31] Much of the argument in book 2, "Creation," centers on establishing that the human soul originated from the creative action of God.[32] Book 3, "Providence," is dominated by discussion of movement: how the human soul moves by choice, how it seeks to move back to its origin and how it tragically fails in that motion.[33] Finally, book 4, "Salvation," depicts the final reunion between humanity and God.

In short, the central dramatic action rejoins what was originally united. If the visual picture of *City of God* is a forked road, then the picture of *Summa contra Gentiles* is a circle. In fact, circle imagery permeates much of Aquinas's other work as a depiction of the ideal motion.[34] The grand reunion between humankind and God encompasses all other reunions

---

[29]Charles Taylor, *Sources of the Self: The Making of the Modern Identity* (Cambridge, Mass.: Harvard University Press, 1989), p. 19.

[30]Donald Capps, *The Depleted Self* (Minneapolis: Fortress, 1993); see also J. Richard Middleton and Brian J. Walsh, *Truth Is Stranger Than It Used to Be* (Downers Grove, Ill.: InterVarsity Press, 1995), pp. 46-62. For further insights into the spiritual effects of this "terrible schism in the heart of man," see Leanne Payne, *The Healing Presence* (Grand Rapids, Mich.: Baker, 1995), p. 157.

[31]*SCG* 1.101, pp. 300-304; *SCG* 1.15, pp. 98-100.

[32]*SCG* 2.87.1-6, pp. 293-95.

[33]*SCG* 3.72.1-7, pp. 242-44 (part 1); *SCG* 3.70-74, pp. 70-74 (part 1); and *SCG* 3.53-55, pp. 179-88 (part 1).

[34]For more on the theme of "circulation," see Jan Aertsen, *Nature and Creature: St. Thomas Aquinas's Way of Thought*, trans. H. D. Morton (Leiden: E. J. Brill, 1988).

necessary for knowledge. The rest of this chapter seeks to show how Aquinas drew his work carefully to enter, retell and ultimately capture the challengers in this sweeping encirclement.

### Entering the Challengers' Story

*The broad land.* We have seen that Aquinas enters the Aristotelian story of knowledge through his shared reliance on philosophical reason and the Aristotelian texts. Generally speaking, an epochal challenge consists of a broad worldview; there will be room for the Christian respondent to establish common ground. For instance, Aquinas spends the early part of book 1 demonstrating via reason and Aristotle the truth that God exists and is one.[35] The Muslim, of course, hardly needed to be argued into believing these truths since such propositions constituted the core of Muhammad's proclamation. Aquinas nevertheless goes through the trouble in order to build mutual confidence that reason and Aristotle can serve as an adequate meeting ground.

However, the broadness of the challengers' story can also entrap. Not all of this land can be confidently entered as common ground. By entering, Christian respondents risk wandering into territory where they may get lost and disoriented. Thus respondents cannot enter the story randomly; they need some sort of compass to keep them on confident ground.

Even on truly common ground the respondent must carefully choose which areas are best suited to the "taking every thought captive" strategy. Chess masters know that choosing the most advantageous points of encounter is crucial to any strategy. Among all the possible areas in the challenger's territory, the respondent must seek to shift the encounter to the most favorable ground.

This section will examine how Aquinas carefully stays on confident ground by relying on the compass of reason. Second, the specific issue of "the eternity of creation" is examined as a case study showing how Aquinas's strategy of entrance involves shifting to favorable ground.

---

[35]*SCG* 1.12, p. 83; *SCG* 1.42, pp. 158-64.

### The Compass of Reason

Reading *SCG*, one senses the almost tranquil confidence with which Aquinas seems to move into his challengers' arguments. This confidence stems from his understanding of reason as a reliable tool of navigation. Aquinas used reason as a compass and not as a god. The popular caricature of Aquinas, especially among Protestants, is of a hyperrationalist, as if he placed faith in reason itself to attain knowledge. Nothing could be further from the truth.

Aquinas always recognized that reason serves only as a pointer. Reason, as he put it, "contains, however, certain likenesses of what belongs to faith, and certain preambles to it, as nature is a preamble to grace."[36] As a preamble, reason can only point toward a far greater reality: God. Reason itself relies on faith in this personal God. God himself serves as the guarantor of reason; he is the sure magnetic field that orients the compass, for "in God there is pure truth, with which no falsity or deception can be mingled."[37]

Aquinas does not mean that every exercise of human reason is infallible, any more than every compass is free from defect. However, Aquinas enters the challengers' story with an underlying confidence that philosophical error stems from particular defects in particular exercises of reason, and not in the reliability of reason itself. Such confidence enables him to remain unfazed by threatening aspects of the challengers' story. All Aquinas needs to do is uncover the error in the Islamic philosophers' compass: "And if in what the philosophers have said we come upon something that is contrary to faith, this does not belong to philosophy but is rather an abuse of philosophy arising from a defect in reason."[38]

The magnetic relationship between human reason and God also points Aquinas to where the defect most likely lies. He demonstrates that God's reasoning process is not "ratiocinative or discursive." In other words, the eternal God knows truth simultaneously as an organic whole: God does not need to string together one principle after another in order to arrive

---

[36]Quoted in Pegis, introduction to *SCG* 1, p. 25.
[37]*SCG* 1.61.1, p. 205.
[38]Quoted in Pegis, introduction to *SCG* 1, p. 25.

at a conclusion.[39] In contrast, human beings' reasoning must attach to first principles an ensuing string of derived conclusions, in much the same way a series of metal pieces can be connected to a magnet. Rational errors occur when people have made inappropriate connections. Aquinas explains: "The intellect does not err in the case of first principles; it errs at times in the case of conclusions at which it arrives by reasoning from first principles. But the divine intellect, as we have shown above, is not ratiocinative or discursive. Therefore there cannot be falsity or deception in it."[40]

This confidence in the reliability of reason is another reason the *SCG* is such a painstakingly complex work. When Aquinas enters the challengers' story and encounters a troubling aspect, he believes that he can uncover where the magnetic power of reason broke down in the challengers' argument. In many cases he will devote dozens of pages to isolating one error.

In this confidence Aquinas shares a strong virtue with Augustine. Just as Augustine believed his God to be the God of history, Aquinas believes his God to be the God of reason. "Now, the knowledge of the principles that are known to us naturally has been implanted in us by God," Aquinas insists, "for God is the Author of our nature."[41] Armed with such belief, both move with confidence that they can properly enter and retell the challengers' story.

Both Augustine and Aquinas also relate either human historical events or human rational processes to the true history or reason that is God's. Just as human historical events are merely "syllables" pointing to the Logos of history, so human reasoning is merely a string of "preambles" to the One who claims to be Truth. In other words, just as Augustine simultaneously values and relativizes history in relation to Christ, so Aquinas simultaneously values and relativizes reason.

The importance of this sort of measured valuation of reason is especially crucial in our epoch. The relativization of reason is a dominant feature of the postmodern epoch. Postmodernism strenuously rejects

---

[39]*SCG* 1.57, pp. 196-99.
[40]*SCG* 1.61.4, pp. 205-6.
[41]*SCG* 1.7.2, p. 74.

modernity's exaltation of the compass of reason. However, the widely observed feeling of "drift" in the postmodern epoch stems from its failure to unravel the true error in modernity. Modernity reached its idolatrous conclusion by following a long line of philosophical reasoning that eventually separated its practice of reason from its original First Principle. It exalted reason by progressively draining the compass of any relationship to God in Christ.[42] Postmodernism has rejected modernity's worship of reason but has unfortunately repeated modernity's underlying error of discharging the compass from its attraction to the Divine North. We Christians can certainly establish common ground with the postmodern challenger in our shared rejection of the worship of reason.[43] But we must discern how to retain the God-given compass. Otherwise we risk getting lost in postmodernity's headlong drift into irrationality.

### Case Study: Shifting to Favorable Ground

The compass of reason also indicated to Aquinas the boundaries of his grounds of confidence. He realized that there was territory in the challengers' story where reason could not guide him. In matters of faith, he repeats over and over in *SCG*, "the natural reason has its failing."[44] In those places he never tries to meet his opponents in a decisive encounter. Instead he seeks to shift the encounter to the ground of his choosing.

An excellent example of this aspect of Aquinas's entrance strategy can be found in the conflict over the "eternity of the world." Islamic commentators claimed that rational argument flowing out of Aristotle's proof of the Prime Mover conclusively demonstrated that the "realm of mobile being has always been."[45] While the specifics of the argument are too

---

[42]See John Milbank, *Theology and Social Theory: Beyond Secular Reason* (Oxford: Blackwell, 1990); and Buckley, *At the Origins of Modern Atheism,* for truly epic tales that unravel how this happened. Both also make the fascinating and persuasive argument that the decisive (and faulty) steps of reasoning were actually provided by Christian theologians and philosophers.

[43]J. Bottum has made this point articulately in "Christians and Postmoderns," *First Things,* February 1994, pp. 28-32.

[44]*SCG* 1.2.3, p. 62.

[45]Quoted in McInerny, *St. Thomas Aquinas,* p. 31. See also David B. Burrell, "Aquinas and Islamic and Jewish Thinkers," in *The Cambridge Companion to Aquinas,* ed. Norman Kretzmann and Eleonore Stump (Cambridge: Cambridge University Press, 1993), pp. 71-75.

complicated to discuss here, the basic challenge came in the assertion that the proof of God's own existence necessitated the conclusion that creation always existed.[46]

Such a conclusion obviously challenged the Christian doctrine of God's creation of the world at a specific time. Aquinas clearly believes that the doctrine of the eternity of the world is "incompatible with the Catholic faith."[47] But he does not attack Averroës's doctrine directly. Instead he painstakingly unravels Averroës's line of reasoning to reveal that the Islamic philosopher's logic "issues in no necessary conclusions." He repeatedly insists that he has not rationally disproved his challengers' doctrine, only that the challengers lacked necessary demonstration of the world's eternity.[48]

Then he makes a very surprising move. At length, he demonstrates that the proofs for "creation in time" offered by the Christian side equally "lack absolute and necessary conclusiveness." In fact he suggests that Christians drop such proofs when contending with nonbelievers, lest opponents think the Catholic faith rests on "ineffectual reasoning."[49] Aquinas demonstrates that this issue is an incommensurable matter of faith: neither side can conclusively persuade the other by resort to the shared authority of reason. Like a grand chess master, he looks ahead and sees that if he engages with the opponent on this area of the board, the result will be an unsatisfying draw.

Instead Aquinas moves the whole discussion of creation to an adjacent part of the board: "However, a more effective approach . . . can be made from the point of view of the end of the divine will. . . . For this fact shows clearly that these things owe their existence to Him, and also is proof that God does not act by a necessity of His nature, and that His power of acting is infinite."[50] In other words, Aquinas wants to move the contest to the question of whether creation was necessary to God or whether it originated out of an act of God's free will. Averroës had claimed that the world

---

[46]See McInerny, *St. Thomas Aquinas*, pp. 31-33.
[47]*SCG* 2.38.16, p. 115.
[48]*SCG* 2.35.1, p. 102.
[49]*SCG* 2.38.8, p. 113.
[50]*SCG* 2.38.15, pp. 114-15.

was eternally necessary because God intrinsically needs a world in order
to exist as an intellect. Once again the line of reasoning is complex, but
the basic argument is that God needs to reason via created beings, and
since God is an eternal intellect, creation and created beings were eternally "necessary" to God. According to Averroës's reasoning, God did not
freely choose to create the world in general and humanity in particular.

Aquinas thus shifts the encounter from a conflict over time (is creation
eternal or not?) to a conflict over God's character (did God create out of
free will or out of necessity?). On this terrain Aquinas is confident that he
can marshal reason and Aristotle to achieve a decisive outcome. Starting
from a previously proved point that "creation is an action proper to God,
and that He alone can create,"[51] he reasons step by step, with help from
Aristotle's own texts (not just Averroës's interpretation), that "it follows
that God acts, in the realm of created things, not by necessity of His
nature, but by the free choice of His will."[52]

His moves surrounding the eternity of the world should alert us that
Aquinas indeed possesses a much more foresighted strategy than simply
defending every aspect of Christianity against every attack. As we shall
see, developing the character of God as a freely choosing Creator is much
more important than establishing the temporal nature of creation; the
former is crucial to a dramatic climax, the latter is incidental. Aquinas
knows God's character is the crucial territory because he anticipates the
need for the gospel, a narrative that features Christ as the complete repre-
sentation of divine character. So even while at this stage Aquinas explicitly restricts himself to the challengers' terms, he implicitly relies on the
gospel to guide his moves.

When readers first try to follow Aquinas, many (like myself) are
tempted to lose interest because of his laborious pace; oxlike, he seems to
stop and chew over every fine blade of distinction, pondering dull
abstractions. But it slowly dawns on the reader that this Dumb Ox is play-
ing an incredible chess game in his mind, thinking hundreds of moves

---

[51]*SCG* 2.21.1, p. 60.
[52]*SCG* 2.23.1, p. 68. Aquinas also demonstrates in this section that it is possible to believe
God freely willed creation *and* still accept the eternity of the world (even though he himself holds the orthodox position that creation occurred in time).

ahead and maneuvering to gain the most favorable ground.

Such foresight stands out in the history of Christian responses to epochal challenges, which unfortunately is littered with wrong battles being fought on unfavorable parts of the board. In the modern era, for instance, opponents used the language of modern science to challenge the Bible as unreliable. They pointed to factual errors in the Bible, the findings of textual criticism, and historical criticism on issues of authorship. An influential Christian strategy of response, led by B. B. Warfield, Charles Hodge and the "Princeton School," reacted to the scientific challenge by trying to defend a rather narrow corner of Christian turf. They developed an account of the Bible that required a rigid defense of the Bible's total factual inerrancy, located scriptural authority as inhering in the actual words of the text, and pointed to the historical moment when each biblical author first wrote down his original text under inspiration.[53] The resulting "battle for the Bible"[54] between these Christians and their challengers degenerated into an "incommensurable" and irresolvable shouting match.

But the turf these modernist Christians staked out was not that which the church throughout history had seen as constituting the crucial ground. From the early church fathers to Augustine to Luther and beyond, the church focused on Scripture's authoritativeness and not total factual inerrancy, scriptural authority that inhered in the Word toward which the text pointed (and not the text itself), and the crucial historical events of the Bible being the actual incarnation, crucifixion and resurrection, and not some hypothetical "moment of inspiration and composition."[55] The Princeton School's poor choice of a meeting ground impoverished not only its encounter with modernity but also the church's legacy to our current epoch. To the extent that such a legacy still dominates how significant portions of the church use the Bible to teach, preach and evangelize, Christians are ill-equipped to translate Scripture

---

[53]John Goldingay, *Models for Scripture* (Grand Rapids, Mich.: Eerdmans, 1994), pp. 261-83.

[54]The phrase is taken from Harold Lindsell's *The Battle for the Bible* (Grand Rapids, Mich.: Zondervan, 1976).

[55]See Donald G. Bloesch, *Holy Scripture: Revelation, Inspiration and Interpretation* (Downers Grove, Ill.: InterVarsity Press, 1994), especially pp. 86-140.

into an effective voice to postmoderns. Under this legacy, Christian rhetoric toward nonbelievers sounds polemical and incomprehensible, something along the lines of "Believe me when I claim the Bible is true because the Bible and I say so."

Furthermore, as the Princeton School and other members of the fundamentalist wing of Christianity expended almost all their intellectual energy on defending their particular account of Scripture, they forsook any real interest in seriously entering the scientific story that best summed up the epochal challenge: namely, Darwinian evolutionary theory. Recent Christian scholarship has revealed how a strategy of entering—and significantly reinterpreting—the Darwinian narrative could have established genuine points of encounter on the turf of science.[56] But most conservative Christians, fearful of losing any more territory, defensively withdrew further into their corner, a corner that became a dead end for any genuine rhetorical and intellectual engagement with science.

In contrast, Aquinas refuses to be drawn into destructive stalemates. He seeks a far greater prize than the mere preservation of each small piece of Christian territory. He will even sacrifice some minor pawns if that will help him cross the boundary into the challengers' territory. And he will plod irresistibly toward a rather peculiar checkmate.

### Retelling the Challengers' Story

Retelling the challengers' story into a tragedy requires an understanding of the key components of tragedy. In Aristotle's *Poetics* the classic treatment of tragic drama, the Greek philosopher turned theater critic emphasized that dramatic action "involves agents, who must necessarily have their distinctive qualities both of character and thought, since it is from these that we ascribe certain qualities to their actions."[57] Character development, in other words, is crucial to correctly interpreting all drama.

---

[56]For some excellent examples, see Michael Behe, *Darwin's Black Box: The Biochemical Challenge to Evolution* (New York: Simon & Schuster, 1998); William Dembski, *The Design Inference* (Cambridge: Cambridge University Press, 1998); Phillip Johnson, *Darwin on Trial* (Downers Grove, Ill.: InterVarsity Press, 1991).

[57]Aristotle *Poetics* 6.1, in *The Works of Aristotle*, trans. W. D. Ross (London: Oxford University Press, 1949), p. 631.

Tragedies generally establish the core natures of the actors early on, because character—the combination of desires and fears, capabilities and limitations—drives the logic of the entire narrative. The actor must remain consistent to the already established character:

> The right thing, however, is in the Characters just as in the incidents of the play to endeavour always after the necessary or the probable; so that whenever such and such a personage says or does such and such a thing, it shall be the necessary or probable outcome of his character; and whenever this incident follows on that, it shall be either the necessary or the probable consequence of it.[58]

For a character in a tragedy, then, one incident follows another to form the narrative trajectory until the tragic incident reveals the "necessary or probable outcome of his character."

In *SCG* the main characters are God and humankind. Aquinas develops these characters for his epic tragedy, but does so by reworking the cast from the challengers' own story. Having entered the Aristotelian narrative, he corrects its characters "from the inside" so that they will be suitable for incorporation into his own gospel metanarrative. Aquinas explains his intentions in his preface: "Now, while we are investigating some given truth, we shall also show what errors are set aside by it; and we shall likewise show how the truth that we come to know by demonstration is in accord with the Christian religion."[59] This section will examine some main examples of his retellings, as well as how Aquinas sets up a trajectory toward the tragic crisis.

*Character development of God.* Aquinas enters the Aristotelian story at a particular locale in order to reveal God as a free creator. God did not need to create human beings, but generously gave humans an inheritance of life, intellect and movement. This will be crucial for Aquinas's epic tale of reunion. As in the parable of the prodigal son, resolution of the tragedy depends on the generous character of the Father.

A similar example of correction involves the depiction of God's knowledge. The Islamic commentators had portrayed God as not knowing par-

---

[58]Aristotle *Poetics* 15, pp. 643-44.
[59]*SCG* 1.2.4, pp. 62-63.

ticulars, which means God does not directly know any individual person's soul. According to James Anderson, they "advocated theories which excluded any real relationship to God by placing man's ultimate end in a union with a separate intellect which is not God, God being conceived as an utterly transcendent entity that must ever remain in its ineffable unity inaccessible to the human spirit."[60] The "separate intellect," known as the Tenth Intelligence, served as God's means of knowledge but was not God himself.

Aquinas rigorously corrects this conception of God. Drawing on several elaborate lines of abstract reasoning that occupy chapters 49-59 of book 1, he demonstrates that we must see God as One who does know particulars. Establishing that God's character knows every individual soul will be crucial to Aquinas's metanarrative. This is because in the Aristotelian framework, the act of knowing is closely related to the act of loving. A subject's intellectual apprehension of an object intimately unites the subject to the object: as nonrational beings unite "by way of assimilation, so intellectual substances do so by way of cognition."[61] So if God and humankind are to reunite lovingly and totally, there must exist real knowledge between the two. On God's end at least, such intimate knowledge is part of his character.

The intimate nature of true knowledge also explains the subsequent rhetorical move in book 1. In chapters 49-59 it appears that Aquinas has already used abstract reason to prove conclusively his case about God's knowledge. He has seemingly considered every conceivable objection and refuted all opposing lines of reasoning. Four chapters later, however, he seems to repeat himself by taking up the same subject once again, spending the next nine chapters demonstrating all over again what he already has conclusively shown. Why the repetition?

A closer examination reveals that his strategy in chapters 63-71 is different in one significant way. Whereas he has already shown by abstract reason that God knows particulars, he now turns to show that the Islamic commentators arrived at their faulty character portrayal by misreading

---

[60]Anderson, introduction to *SCG* 2, p. 15.
[61]*SCG* 3.25.6, p. 99 (part 1).

some key portions of Aristotle's texts.[62] In the challengers' story, Aristotle was the most beloved authority. Aquinas is thus taking great pains to allow his challengers to continue treasuring a valued part of their story even while being corrected. Like Augustine, Aquinas does not insist that his challengers always abandon their story to be right; on the contrary, he exerts every effort to demonstrate that the seeds of correct character development already lie in their story. Aquinas is committed to knowing Aristotle more completely than his challengers do and thus in a very real sense loving his challengers' story more truly than they do themselves.

The reader feels this appreciation welling up within every page of *Summa contra Gentiles.* Like the Islamic Falasifa, Aquinas honors Aristotle as the "philosopher who knew." But Aquinas cites Aristotle's works even more profusely and reads him even more closely than the vast majority of Islamic scholars do. While most Muslims and Christians alike were content to study Aristotle only through the Falasifa's translations and commentary, Aquinas acquired and pored over several different translations.[63] One gets the strong sense that his hard-earned mastery of Aristotle was not simply motivated by a desire to prove his Islamic opponents wrong but was a genuine labor of love.

*Character development of humankind.* Aristotle declared in *Poetics* that "character in a play is that which reveals the moral purpose of the agents, i.e. the sort of thing they seek or avoid."[64] To develop the character of humanity, Aquinas enlists numerous references to Aristotelian scientists to show that the sought end of every object is its origin.[65] This overarching purpose determines the trajectory of every human being, for it is basic to Aristotle that "a thing is then best disposed when it is fittingly ordered to its end."[66] The natural conclusion follows: the purpose of every individual is to follow a trajectory toward God, since "God is at once the ultimate end of things and the first agent, as we have shown."[67]

---

[62]*SCG* 1.63-71, pp. 209-39. See especially p. 209 n.1
[63]Aertsen, "Aquinas's Philosophy," p. 21.
[64]Aristotle *Poetics* 6.2, p. 633.
[65]*SCG* 3.22, pp. 83-88 (part 1).
[66]*SCG* 1.1.1, p. 59.
[67]*SCG* 3.18.3, p. 74 (part 1)

Our purpose is to trace a movement that is the cosmic dramatic action of "reunite." As an intellectual substance, human beings can fully complete the circle only by knowing God fully, for "a thing is more closely united with God by the fact that it attains to His very substance in some manner, and this is accomplished when one knows something of the divine substance. . . . Therefore, an intellectual substance tends to divine knowledge as an ultimate end."[68]

Aquinas reworks other aspects of the challengers' characterization of humanity. Averroists had claimed that an individual soul does not last through eternity; only a universal soul possesses eternal dimensions. As usual, Aquinas examines Aristotle and the Averroists' own reasoning to isolate their error. As he does so, he also shows that the Averroists convict themselves of error, for they had condemned an ancient school of thought for making essentially the same error he has just uncovered. Their own logic should lead them to conclude that an individual person possesses an eternal soul.[69]

Each of these corrections is made to prepare the challengers' story for its eventual capture by Aquinas's metanarrative. As we saw in the previous chapter, a captivating metanarrative must be a more compelling story. How compelling a story can be depends partly on how weighty the stakes are for the main character: What are the consequences of achieving or failing the protagonist's overarching purpose?[70] For example, suppose the younger son in the parable of the prodigal son did not come to believe his true destination was his father's house, or suppose that his future well-being would not depend on whether he was welcomed home. The parable would hardly seem very compelling. Aquinas is correcting the Aristotelian story to show that every human being's purpose is to return to God and that there are eternal consequences for every individual soul in that journey. The challengers' story must be retold in this way if it is to participate in Aquinas's more compelling metanarrative.

Today's Christian must revise the postmodern epistemological story in similar fashion. Postmoderns like Alex shrug off rival accounts of truth

---

[68]*SCG* 3.25.2, p. 97 (part 1).
[69]*SCG* 1.27.9, p. 134.
[70]See Robert McKee, *Story* (New York: HarperCollins, 1997), pp. 149-52

with a "so what?" because their own epistemological story proposes no real consequences: whether one succeeds in the pursuit of truth doesn't matter in the long run. It is no surprise that postmodern critics frequently describe their own work and indeed all efforts at understanding as mere play.[71] The most immediately needed move, then, does not involve demanding that postmoderns once again adhere to some universal abstract logic; instead we must begin by simply showing that questions of moral truth actually have had higher stakes in their lives than they realize. This requires sympathetically handling their life stories, delicately drawing out the (sometimes painful) consequences of their moral choices that may have long lain hidden even to their own consciousness. Such retellings are necessary to prepare them to take part in the much more compelling gospel story, a story filled with eternal consequences for every individual.

This sort of delicate correction runs throughout *Summa contra Gentiles* and demonstrates the true meaning of *mastery*: adopting a sympathetic yet critical attitude, exerting a sensitive yet firm hand. In the way an artisan masters his craft, Aquinas is seeking to demonstrate that he has mastered Aristotle. In fact, he desires to handle Aristotle's ideas more truly than Aristotle did himself. Commenting on how Aquinas rereads Aristotle to reveal the Christian doctrine of creation, Étienne Gilson (arguably the greatest Thomist scholar of the twentieth century) summarizes Aquinas's attitude thus:

> He [Aquinas] knew very well that Aristotle does not teach [the doctrine of creation], but what interests him is to see and make clear that, although Aristotle did not grasp this capital truth, his principles, while remaining precisely what they are, are perfectly capable of bearing its weight. It is true that for this purpose they have to be deepened in a way that Aristotle did not foresee; but to deepen them thus is merely to bring them into closer conformity with their own essence since it is to make them truer.[72]

---

[71]For example, see Jacques Derrida, *Of Grammatology* (Baltimore: Johns Hopkins University Press, 1977), pp. 152-60.

[72]Étienne Gilson, *The Spirit of Mediaeval Philosophy* (Notre Dame, Ind.: University of Notre Dame Press, 1991), p. 424.

Aquinas has so devoted himself to his challengers' material that he knows it intimately; he can best grasp its dimensions and capabilities.

In the particular retelling of human character as an individual and eternal soul, Aquinas buttresses Aristotle and Averroës so they can bear a heavier load. As the teller of a more compelling story, Aquinas is loading his story with weightier consequences. In any narrative, as the consequences gain weight, the dramatic tension builds—a tension Aquinas intensifies to its crisis point.

*The tragic crisis.* It has become common to associate dramatic tragedy with some tragic flaw in moral character. Many Shakespearean tragedies certainly feature such a fault: for example, the indecisiveness of Hamlet or the perverse ambition of Macbeth. Popular judgments on American political tragedies likewise focus on some persistent moral defect, such as the paranoia that sank Nixon or the lack of self-control that almost ended Clinton's presidency. And as discussed in chapter three, the first half of *City of God* can be read as an exposé of Rome's tragic flaw of pride.

But there also exists a classical conception that attributes tragedy not to moral flaws but rather to epistemological failures. In *Poetics* Aristotle himself argues that a tragic figure is one "whose misfortune, however, is brought upon him not by vice and depravity but by some error of judgment."[73] The discovery of long-held misjudgment or ignorance precipitates the crisis in the tragic plot.[74] *Oedipus Rex* is the paradigmatic example of the tragic crisis as a crisis of knowledge.

Aquinas brings Aristotle's own conception of dramatic tragedy to bear on Aristotle's philosophy, drawing out the hidden epistemological tragedy.[75] The Islamic challengers relied on Aristotelian philosophy to lead one to real knowledge. Undergirding this philosophy was the epistemological judgment that human senses can lead one to real knowledge. The

---

[73]Aristotle *Poetics* 13, p. 640.

[74]Aristotle *Poetics* 11, p. 638.

[75]I have been unable to ascertain whether Aquinas would have had access to Aristotle's *Poetics* at the writing of *SCG*, so I am not necessarily claiming he was using such a conception of tragedy with explicit knowledge that it was Aristotelian. However, it seems reasonable to assume that as one thoroughly steeped in Aristotle, Aquinas would have picked up the Aristotelian mindset on this topic. In any case, my more important point—how Aquinas sets up the "tragic crisis"—is not dependent on these questions.

senses give the human reason adequate access to truth, even truth about the divine. In *Summa contra Gentiles* Aquinas leads his challengers to discover that this is a critical misjudgment.

Aquinas prompts this discovery in a number of ways. His most effective approach involves dissecting exactly what information the senses can comprehend and feed to human reason. He shows that senses only partially grasp "external accidents, which are the proper sensibles—for example color, odor, and the like."[76] As one moves higher up the chain of beings, such "accidents" constitute less and less of the full being. Aquinas points out the problem: "Much less will the intellect arrive at comprehending the natures of those things of which we grasp few accidents by sense; and it will do so even less in the case of those things whose accidents cannot be grasped by the senses."[77]

When the object of knowledge becomes the highest being, the source of all beings and ways, then we must ask: "If, then, we imperfectly know the ways themselves, how shall we be able to arrive at a perfect knowledge of the source of these ways? And because that source transcends the above-mentioned ways beyond proportion, even if we knew the ways themselves perfectly we would yet not have within our grasp a perfect knowledge of the source."[78] Aquinas sums up the limits of sense and reason to know God:

> For, according to its manner of knowing in the present life, the intellect depends on the sense for the origin of knowledge; and so those things that do not fall under the senses cannot be grasped by the human intellect except in so far as the knowledge of them is gathered from sensible things. Now, sensible things cannot lead the human intellect to the point of seeing in them the nature of the divine substance; for sensible things are effects that fall short of the power of their cause.[79]

One must note that these limits are not attributed to some spectacular or even secret moral impropriety. On the contrary, Aristotelian knowers

---

[76]*SCG* 4.1.3, p. 36.
[77]Ibid.
[78]Ibid.
[79]*SCG* 1.3.3, p. 64.

are acting out of the best motivations in human character. They are seeking to know God, their true origin. That these knowers are tracing their
most proper trajectory and yet must fall short of their desired end is the
tragic crisis. Aquinas enlists Aristotle to show in chapter after chapter that
no other sort of knowledge other than knowledge of God can bring
human beings "true felicity."[80] But in fourteen consecutive chapters he
relentlessly demonstrates that by Aristotle's own logic, human reason
simply cannot achieve this felicity.[81]

This rhetorical strategy sounds a very different note from what is
sometimes heard from Christians as they encounter other religions. Lesslie Newbigin, one of the most insightful Christian missiologists of our day
and himself a missionary in India for nearly forty years, comments on the
grating tone of a common approach:

> There is something deeply repulsive in the attitude, sometimes found
> among Christians, which makes only grudging acknowledgment of the
> faith, the godliness, and the nobility to be found in the lives of non-Chris-
> tians. Even more repulsive is the idea that in order to communicate the
> gospel to them one must, as it were, ferret out their hidden sins, show that
> their goodness is not so good after all, as a precondition for presenting the
> offer of grace in Christ.[82]

Unlike the Catholic polemicists of Aquinas's day and numerous Western authors in ours, Aquinas refuses to project all sorts of evils onto the
Eastern "other."[83] He freely acknowledges the nobility of Islamic efforts at
knowledge. But the sincere and good endeavors of Averroës and Avicenna
only point out the tragic limits of human reason and senses.

Aquinas also intensifies the epistemological crisis by showing that the
senses do whet the human appetite for our true end. Even though "sensible things cannot lead the human intellect to the point of seeing," they do
lead us "to the point of knowing about God that He exists. . . . There are,

---

[80]*SCG* 3.63.1-10, pp. 206-9 (part 1).

[81]*SCG* 3.26-42, pp. 103-43 (part 1).

[82]Lesslie Newbigin, *The Gospel in a Pluralist Society* (Grand Rapids, Mich.: Eerdmans,
1989), p. 180.

[83]For a postmodern analysis of this tendency, see Edward Said, *Orientalism* (New York: Pan
theon, 1978).

consequently, some intelligible truths about God that are open to the human reason; but there are others that absolutely surpass power."[84] Human senses operate very much like the compass of reason: they do faintly detect the presence of that vast North, but they themselves cannot transport us there. *SCG* re-creates for humankind Ulysses' tragic state of knowing that his home lies beyond the horizon yet being prevented from discovering the actual way back. This tragedy is foreshadowed from the beginning of the tale: "Sensible things, from which human reason takes the origin of its knowledge, retain within themselves some sort of trace of a likeness to God. This is so imperfect, however, that it is absolutely inadequate to manifest the substance of God."[85]

Aquinas takes every opportunity to evoke the pathos of reason and senses. Pathos is most powerful when certain opposites exist simultaneously in the character, like despondency felt within the shadows of joy, or persistence practiced short of full completion. Aquinas depicts these tragic combinations with all his powers of philosophy. He argues that human reason rightfully persists in its incomplete effort to think about God:

> It is useful for the human reason to exercise itself in such arguments [about God's nature] however weak they may be, provided only that there be present no presumption to comprehend or to demonstrate. For to be able to see something of the loftiest realities, however thin and weak the sight may be, is, as our previous remarks indicate, a cause of the greatest joy.[86]

As much joy as it is "to see something of the loftiest realities," such sights only come with the somber reminder of limitation: "however thin and weak the sight may be." Aquinas even extensively quotes Aristotle himself to recast "the Philosopher who knew" in this tragic mold:

> A still further benefit may also be seen in what Aristotle says in the *Ethics*. There was a certain Simonides who exhorted people to put aside the knowledge of divine things and to apply their talents to human occupa-

---

[84]*SCG* 1.3.3, p. 64.
[85]*SCG* 1.8.1, pp. 75-76.
[86]*SCG* 1.8.1, p. 76.

tions. He said that "he who is a man should know human things, and he
who is mortal, things that are mortal." Against Simonides Aristotle says that
"man should draw himself towards what is immortal and divine as much as
he can." And so he says in the *De animalibus* that, although what we know
of the higher substance is very little, yet that little is loved and desired
more than all the knowledge that we have about less noble substances. He
also says in the *De caelo et mundo* that when questions about the heavenly
bodies can be given even a modest and merely plausible solution, he who
hears this experiences intense joy.[87]

From Aquinas's rendering of the scene, one almost imagines Aristotle listening to "even a modest and merely plausible solution" the way the Tim
Robbins character in the tragic scene from the film *The Shawshank
Redemption* listens to a scratchy recording of Mozart with intense joy, a
joy made poignant by the despondent reality of his imprisonment.

Book 3 especially evokes this poignancy for those who dwell within
the Aristotelian story. Book 3 upholds the great value of Aristotelian sciences. They belong to the realm of "sensible works" that "awaken man
himself to divine matters by these actions."[88] Like the prodigal son in the
pigsty, humanity comes to its senses and remembers its true home. We are
enticed to curve back toward the Person and place of our origin. But
book 3 shows over and over again that such "sensible works" will not
enable us to complete our trajectory to the end. For instance, Aquinas
draws on Aristotelian science to discuss the nature of motion, concluding:

> Besides, as long as anything is in motion toward perfection, it is not yet at
> the ultimate end. But all men, while learning the truth, are always disposed
> as beings in motion, and as tending toward perfection.... Since man's ulti
> mate felicity in this life seems mainly to consist in speculation, whereby the
> knowledge of the truth is sought, as Aristotle himself proves in *Ethics X*, it
> is impossible to say that man achieves his ultimate end in this life.[89]

In other words, a human being's trajectory in life will be doomed to fruitless motion short of completing the circle.

---

[87]*SCG* 1.5.5, pp. 70-71.
[88]*SCG* 3.119.4, p. 131 (part 2).
[89]*SCG* 3.48.12, p. 166 (part 1).

As mentioned in the beginning of this chapter, some modern scholars have difficulty believing that *Summa contra Gentiles* was composed for the historical issues facing a Dominican missionary to Islam. Some of Aquinas's contemporaries undoubtedly read the work with the same puzzlement. Aquinas's discussions seem always to fly to universal and timeless heights. In place of critiques of specific Islamic doctrines or any discussion of the contemporary conflicts between Christian and Islamic people, we have the discovery of the universal limits of human knowledge and the tragic character of humanity. On the surface Aquinas seems to have once again drifted away into the realms of abstraction, dreamily oblivious to requests for a practical strategy.

But it is precisely this abstraction that expresses the brilliance of Aquinas's strategy. By eschewing polemics against Islamic doctrine and staying on common ground, Aquinas has placed himself as a fellow sufferer in the tragic crisis he unfolds. Unlike the Only City epochal story with its emphasis on the epistemological superiority of a specific Christian civilization, the epistemological tragedy Aquinas recounts applies equally to all civilizations. Left by itself, the story of human reason is too constricted for everyone: "If the only way open to us for the knowledge of God were solely that of the reason, the human race would remain in the blackest shadows of ignorance."[90]

The Christian knower shares the same limitations of human reason and senses as Aristotle, Averroës and Avicenna. Aquinas has entered the challengers' story—a story that could have been simply told and received as a story of Islam against Christianity—and has rewritten it into a fully human tragedy.

### Capturing the Challengers

Aquinas now is ready to tell his carefully crafted presentation of the gospel. This metanarrative will capture challengers by proving to be a wider, more compelling and ultimately more experiential tale. In each of these ways Aquinas seeks to narrate the conclusion of the human story. The gospel will resolve ways humanity has gotten tragically stuck short of

---

[90]*SCG* 1.4.4, p. 67.

the complete reunion it so desperately desires.

*A wider narrative.* Aquinas first wakens challengers to the possibility that there exists a wider world than their own. He has already pointed the way with his use of reason as a compass: reason makes sense only when oriented to a faith in a transcendent realm. A few other examples demonstrate how he continually seeks to widen his challengers' vision of an unseen land.

The challengers' experiences are framed as symptoms of dwelling in a constricted story. An excellent example of this is found in chapters 122-27 in book 3, part 2. At first glance it seems Aquinas is making one of those confusing moves that have led scholars to wonder about the unity of the entire work. In these chapters he suddenly leaves abstract issues to give a frank and detailed analysis of sexual activity and food. In the beginning of the section he states that his practical assessments are based on the philosophical point he has just proved.[91] The point he has just proved is how the "improper use of [corporeal and sensible things] either completely distracts the mind from God, and so the end of the will is fixed in inferior things, or such abuse slows down the inclination of the mind toward God so that we become attached to things of this kind to an extent greater than is necessary."[92] He then analyzes the end result when one "set[s] the end of his will in these things [sex and food]."[93]

Aquinas thus provides an explanation for the common phenomenon of addiction. He interprets the Muslim endorsement of polygamy as evidence for the general male desire for ever more sexual experiences, a desire that refuses to be satiated by natural limits. He also reads some Islamic doctrines as allowing the unrestrained consumption of food.[94] Aquinas thus assumes that Muslims would especially experience the general human tendency to addiction, especially to sex and food. Whether rates of addiction were actually higher in Islamic societies is not the point here (although I doubt that they were); the important insight is that he is

---

[91]*SCG* 3.122.1, p. 142 (part 2).
[92]*SCG* 3.121.1, p. 141 (part 2).
[93]*SCG* 3.127.7, p. 158 (part 2).
[94]See *SCG* 1.6.4, pp. 73-74. See Waltz, "Muhammad and the Muslims," for more on this perspective which was widely shared by most Christians.

attempting to explain the challengers' experiences better with his own story. Assuming that Muslims did experience a high degree of addiction as they lived out the beliefs of their story, Aquinas is showing how that particular experience makes sense only in his metanarrative. In other words, he places his challengers in a more coherent and wider story. Addicts understand addiction only when they realize that they are caught in the wrong circle. If the challengers do not join Aquinas's wider picture of reuniting with God, they will remain trapped in the viciously shrinking cycle of attachment to lesser things.

Aquinas wants to show how such addiction tragically limits human experience. So he paints one picture after another of a place where human hungers are truly satisfied. Indeed, he takes the very terms of addiction and recasts them in the light of God's final banquet:

> If, therefore, the goodness, beauty, and delightfulness of creatures are so alluring to the minds of men, the fountainhead of God's own goodness, compared with the rivulets of goodness found in creatures, will draw the enkindled minds of men wholly to Itself. . . . And elsewhere it is written concerning the children of men: "They shall be inebriated with the plenty of Thy house."[95]

In Aquinas's metanarrative even an experience as base as addiction should lead us to long for God.

The genius of this strategy is especially evident when one thinks about the current postmodern generation. Sexual and food addictions have run rampant while remaining poorly understood—a contradiction that postmodernism itself cannot quite explain. However, the Christian metanarrative Aquinas provides can explain both the symptom of addiction and its internal inexplicability: postmoderns' addiction to lower things results from the removal of God as an object of the will; postmoderns' lack of explanation stems from the removal of God from their viciously shrinking story.[96] Not only that but Aquinas shows that all desires can be resolved only in the gospel. As Alasdair MacIntyre has put it, Aquinas's general strategy is to challenge his challengers: "Tell me

---

[95]*SCG* 2.2.4, p. 31.
[96]See Gerald May, *Addiction and Grace* (San Francisco: HarperCollins, 1988), pp. 2-20

your story and I will show you that it only becomes intelligible within this framework."[97]

Aquinas also suggests that he possesses a wider story by giving his challengers a limited role within his broader tale. In the few places where Aquinas does discuss Islamic doctrine, he almost always places its errors next to other false teachings—Manichaeism, Arianism and others that have faced the church through its long history.[98] For instance, after his refutation of finding felicity in carnality, he concludes: "Also refuted is the error of the Cerinthians . . . Chiliasts; that is, Millenarians. Refuted too, are the fables of the Jews and the Saracens."[99] He wants to convey the sense that Islamic teaching is nothing new, surprising or ultimately world-shaking. Instead Islam can easily be located within the wider perspective of the church's own story. I believe this is yet another reason Aquinas does not discuss Islam itself at length. As Augustine did vis-à-vis the myth of Rome, Aquinas indirectly strips away Islam's pretensions of uniqueness. The challengers may conceive of their story as a broad land, but there exists a far vaster continent that could embrace them and their story whole.

In this strategic move Aquinas was virtually alone among his contemporaries. Christians who bothered to ponder the Islamic challenge at length invariably tended to be hypnotized by its threatening arrival on the world stage. As a result, they assigned the challengers special status in their version of the Christian story. For instance, Joachim of Fiore constructed an entire eschatology that featured Islam as one of the "beast heads" in the Apocalypse.[100] Even Humbert of Romans, himself a master in the Dominican order, eventually succumbed to the belief that the Saracens were the most dangerous persecutors ever faced by the church. Unless they are destroyed by military power, he warned, the "Saracens will persevere forever." Not surprisingly, such warnings became a "weighty authority for the justification of crusade," rousing Christians to

---

[97]MacIntyre, *Three Rival Versions*, p. 125.

[98]For instance, see *SCG* 1.42.23-24, p. 164.

[99]*SCG* 3.27.11-13, p. 113 (part 1).

[100]Benjamin Z. Kedar, *Crusade and Mission* (Princeton, N.J.: Princeton University Press, 1984), pp. 112-16.

defend the Holy Land.[101] Ironically, by giving the Islamic challengers this apocalyptic role, men like Joachim of Fiore and Humbert of Romans had already surrendered the church's most holy territory: the gospel metanarrative. Islam had so invaded these Christians' story that the challengers occupied key landmarks like the story's very conclusion.

Aquinas never surrenders this most sacred ground. Instead he weaves the biblical metanarrative into his discussion in order to capture his challengers. On just about every issue he demonstrates that "this truth that we have proved is likewise strengthened by the authority of Sacred Scripture."[102] At the end of almost every chapter he ends his lengthy rational arguments by citing Scripture that pithily summarizes the conclusion just derived. To borrow Robert Jastrow's famous depiction of modern cosmological research, Aquinas paints a picture of reason laboriously scaling every high mountain only to find on every single peak the biblical authors sitting and waiting expectantly.[103] Indeed, the sheer span of the biblical narrative hints at a vast North that looms over the horizon. And if seekers will only lift their eyes, they will see Someone coming.

*A more compelling tale.* When book 4 opens, references to Aristotle drop off precipitously, technical terms of philosophy fade, and the biblical story assumes center stage. Aquinas has already prepared the audience for its arrival: the challengers' confidence in sense and reason has tragically collapsed in on itself. As he summarizes his arguments so far, "There is abundant evidence of how even the brilliant minds of these men suffered from the narrowness of their viewpoint."[104] Only another tale can provide a way to continue the story of knowledge. In the foreword to book 4, Aquinas introduces the points he will make. "Nonetheless, that no presumption of knowing perfectly may be present, points of this kind must be proved from sacred Scripture, but not from natural reason."[105]

His version of the biblical metanarrative starts with the internal nature of God in the Trinity, taking special care to establish the divinity of Jesus

---

[101]Ibid., p. 184.
[102]*SCG* 1.65.11, p. 216.
[103]Robert Jastrow, *God and the Astronomers* (New York: W. W. Norton, 1978).
[104]*SCG* 3.48.15, p. 167 (part 1).
[105]*SCG* 4.1.10, p. 39.

Christ.[106] The story of God builds to its climax in chapter 27. Aquinas announces:

> It now remains to speak of the Incarnation itself. Indeed, among divine works, this most especially exceeds the reason: for nothing can be thought of which is more marvelous than this divine accomplishment: that the true God, the Son of God, should become true man. And because among them all it is most marvelous, it follows that toward faith in this particular marvel all other miracles are ordered.[107]

Indeed, taking a step back to see the whole narrative flow of the *SCG*, we can see how and why the work has been brilliantly ordered toward this point.

In Christian preaching the incarnation was the doctrine Islam rejected most immediately. It was considered outrageous blasphemy and dismissed out of hand without further consideration. But now, after Aquinas has entered and retold the challengers' story, the incarnation becomes the one Christian belief that most completes the Aristotelian story of knowledge. The incarnation completes the circle. If human senses so tragically fall short of reaching God, then God himself kindly reaches out to human senses.

The climactic act of reunion compels because it resolves the tragic crisis. In his introduction to the incarnation, Aquinas makes sure to evoke again the despondency of the Aristotelian seeker: "For we have shown in Book III that the perfect beatitude of man consists in the immediate vision of God. It might, of course, appear to some that man would never have the ability to achieve this state . . . for there is an unmeasured distance between the natures, and thus, in the search for beatitude, a man would grow cold, held back by very desperation." Thankfully, Aquinas continues, "The fact that God was willing to unite human nature to Himself personally points out to men with greatest clarity that man can be united to God by intellect, and see Him immediately . . . stir[ring] up man's hope for beatitude."[108] This climax captures the audience's deepest desires.

---

[106]*SCG* 4.3-12, pp. 42-92.
[107]*SCG* 4.27.1, p. 147.
[108]*SCG* 4.54.2, p. 228.

The incarnation flows "personally" out of the corrected character portrayal of God. Just as the freely offered generosity of God was revealed in creation, so his "superabundant goodness" is witnessed in his descent into that creation.[109] The incarnation thus unites the intellect's knowledge of God with the heart's love for God: "Nothing, of course, so induces us to love one as the experience of his love for us. But God's love for men could be demonstrated to man in no way more effective than this: he willed to be united to man in person, for it is proper to love to unite the love with the beloved so far as possible."[110] God's true character is revealed not just as the Prime Mover or the First Cause but as the loving Father who, when his prodigal children cannot find their way home, comes running out to reunite himself with his offspring. This God created, knows and holds humanity in his arms.

Aquinas has thought through every one of his chess moves with this end in mind. He has crossed the boundary lines to engage with the challenger. He has maneuvered to reveal a huge gap in his opponent's arrangement. But his end game turns out to be no ordinary chess strategy. He will not seek victory by eliminating his challenger's pieces one by one and triumphantly knocking over the opposing king. Instead he engages with his opponent in such a way as to join together all the pieces on the board, encircling everyone in a shared desire for a missing piece. And then Aquinas tells his captivating tale of the true King who descends from above to fill the gap.

The incarnation is God's response to us when we stumble about in the midst of an epochal challenge. It is the incarnate One that we are groping for when we vaguely sense something is missing. Jesus Christ is the One we cling to when disorienting forces pull us in conflicting directions. In our age those forces seem to pull from within the very self; they threaten to disintegrate the unity of the human person.

The mind that slavishly builds more advanced microprocessors to calculate answers even faster is the same mind that whispers that there is no objective truth. The senses to which modern philosophers deny any access to objective reality are the same senses that the media seek to sat-

---

[109]*SCG* 4.1.4, p. 36.
[110]*SCG* 4.54.5, pp. 230-31.

urate. The body that is treated as nothing more than an outcome of ran
dom genetic processes and various chemical reactions is the same body
that is worshiped and glorified by the culture. The postmodern epoch that
celebrates "difference" lacks any reality that can hold all these disparate
forces together in one human being. Whipsawed this way and that, a postmodern person like Alex does not know which way to look.

Standing some seven centuries earlier, amidst the ancestors of these
very forces of disintegration, Aquinas knew which direction to look. It was
not within some self-constructed reality, but above, from a wider land.
Only from heaven above descends the Christ who reunites all. Only the
incarnation provides a person who holds all realities—indeed Reality
itself—together in one human being.

*A more experiential tale.* In Aquinas's metanarrative of knowledge, then,
epistemological surety is gained not by splitting reality into ever more fragmented shards but in reunion with a Person. Jesus Christ is God's personal
guarantor of true knowledge. Since this knowledge comes only through this
personal relationship, it follows that all knowledge is also deeply experiential and personal. Postmodern people may delude themselves into thinking
that they are making up in their own heads some abstract form of logic, but
even they must acknowledge their experience of another person. And the
experience of all "personal knowledge," as Michael Polanyi has persuasively argued, requires the risk of faith.[111]

Echoing Augustine's famous dictum *credo ut intelligam* ("I believe
that I may understand"), Aquinas reminds the reader of the necessity of
faith to begin any epistemological story. "Knowledge must be through
faith," Aquinas insists. "When a person is being taught by a teacher, he
must at the start accept the teacher's conceptions, not as one who under-
stands them by himself, but by way of belief."[112]

This personal faith drives the epistemological story along its true trajectory:

---

[111]Michael Polanyi, *Science, Faith and Society* (Chicago: University of Chicago Press, 1964).
    For the application of Polanyi's work in science to theology, see Lesslie Newbigin, *Proper
    Confidence: Faith, Doubt and Certainty in Christian Discipleship* (Grand Rapids, Mich.:
    Eerdmans, 1995), pp. 1-15; and Newbigin, *Gospel in a Pluralist Society*, pp. 43-48.
[112]*SCG* 3.152.4, p. 236.

Since man's perfect beatitude, furthermore, consists in the sort of knowledge of God which exceeds the capacity of every created intellect (as was
shown in Book III), there had to be a certain foretaste of this sort of knowledge in man which might direct him to that fullness of blessed knowledge;
and this done through faith.[113]

Between the beginning and the conclusion, faith is required at every step
because the "fullness of blessed knowledge" still "exceeds the capacity of
every created intellect" in our lifetimes.

So we place our faith in Jesus Christ, believing that as we unite ourselves more fully to him we will be carried up into ever greater experiences of truth. Again the incarnation serves as a personal promise that
this journey will be completed: the One who shared mortality and limited
senses with humanity will also share his immortality and transcendence
of sense. Aquinas describes this promise:

Therefore, these things are so revealed to man as, for all that, not to be
understood but only to be believed as heard, for the human intellect in this
state in which it is connected with things sensible cannot be elevated
entirely to gaze upon things which exceed every proportion of sense. But,
when it shall have been freed from the connection with the sensibles, then
it will be elevated to gaze upon the things which are revealed.[114]

An unimaginable final feast with the Father awaits us, but we must travel
by faith on this journey home.

We who have received Christ testify to how this journey is filled with
what Aquinas called "a certain foretaste of this sort of knowledge." We
who believe already partake of the appetizers of this final feast. This is
why in the final book of *Summa contra Gentiles*, between the topics of
incarnation and resurrection (which ends the entire work), each of the
intervening twenty-three chapters deals with the church's sacraments.
These physical, tangible, bodily acts, when taken in faith and breathed on
by the Spirit, lead to ever fuller experiences of our God. The sacraments,
especially the Eucharist, are ever-increasing tastes of a final feast with
Father, Son and Holy Spirit.

---

[113]*SCG* 4.54.4, p. 229.
[114]*SCG* 4.1.4, p. 37.

Thus the beginning, the ongoing journey and the final culmination of this epistemological metanarrative are experiences of a personal reunion. All aspects of the person—body and mind, head and heart, sense and intellect—are increasingly reintegrated with each other as the person more fully reunites with God himself. The final paragraph of Aquinas's epic issues an invitation to everyone to look forward to the final reunion that reconciles all reality:

> Since, then, the bodily creation will at the last be disposed in harmony with the state of man—since men, of course, will not only be freed from corruption but also clothed with glory, as what has been said makes clear—necessarily even the bodily creation will achieve a kind of resplendence in its own way. And, hence the saying of the Apocalypse (21:1): "I saw a new heaven and a new earth." And Isaias (65:17-18): "Behold I create new heavens, and a new earth: and the former things shall not be in remembrance and they shall not come upon the heart. But you shall be glad and rejoice forever." Amen.[115]

In the end the story Aquinas tells is not an abstract philosophy or a rational structure. It is an experiential tale into which all are invited. Aquinas himself was captivated by this tale and longed for its conclusion. Every morning he would rise early and ascend to a place of prayer, often on a height overlooking valleys. There, in deep contemplation, he would surrender himself to this wider, more compelling and ever more experiential story. Often he would silently recite a poem he composed. Reading the poem, one glimpses a vision of what Thomas imagined lay ahead:

> O God of every consolation,
> you who find in us nothing you have not given,
> on you I call:
> After this life has reached its ending
> may you be pleased to give me
> knowledge of the first truth
> and my will's fulfilment in your majesty divine.
>
> Most generous rewarder:
> Give my body, too,

---

[115]*SCG* 4.97.7-8, p. 349.

the beauty of lightsomeness,
responsiveness of flesh to spirit,
fit readiness in glorified perfection,
assurance free from fear of harm.

And may you add to these
an overflow of riches,
inflow of delights,
confluence of goods,
so that
I may rejoice
in your consolation above me,
your land's loveliness beneath me,
soul and body's glorification within me,
friends human and angel delightfully around me.

Most merciful Father:
There with you
may I attain
in my reason, wisdom's light,
in my desire, possession of true goods,
in my striving, triumph's honour—

With you:
all dangers gone,
the dwellings various,
all wills harmonious;
where there is
springtime loveliness,
summer brightness,
autumn's plenty,
winter rest.

Lord God:
Give life without death,
joy without sorrow,
where there is

highest liberty,
liberation from all cares,
carefree tranquillity,
joyful happiness,
happy eternity,
eternal blessedness,
the sight and praise of truth:
God.
Amen[116]

Thomas Aquinas was eventually declared a saint by the Catholic Church not just because of his extraordinary thoughts but because of his extraordinary experiences. His contemporaries testified that in his prayers he had experienced God in visions, sounds and even in bodily sensations. For all the energy he poured into his philosophy, he knew that a single experience with the God of creation, incarnation and resurrection radically relativized all his thoughts.

In December 1273 after one extraordinary celebration of Mass, Aquinas suddenly stopped his prodigious flow of writing. When Reginald of Piperno, his friend and secretary, asked why, he answered simply, "I can write no more." When Reginald pressed him for an explanation, Aquinas repeated: "I can write no more. I have seen things which make all my writings like straw." He never wrote another work, leaving unfinished his most famous masterpiece, *Summa Theologica.*

Shortly after this experience, the pope requested his presence at the historic Council of Lyons. He embarked on the long journey by foot. Still miles short of his destination, he suddenly fell gravely ill. He was taken to a nearby monastery, received the last sacraments and then completed his journey to his true Home, his true Feast.[117]

---

[116]Cited and translated by Finnis, *Aquinas,* pp. 333-34.
[117]Kretzmann, "Thomas Aquinas," p. 333. See also Pegis, introduction to *SCG* 1, p. 16; and Chesterton, *Saint Thomas Aquinas,* p. 141.

# 5

# Conclusion
## LEGACIES & LESSONS

THE STRATEGY OF "TAKING EVERY THOUGHT CAPTIVE" offers a unifying interpretation of the *City of God* and *Summa contra Gentiles*. I hope my readings have provided fresh insight into how each of these classics coheres as an individual work, and that my comparative analysis reveals a deeper unity between these two monuments of Christian thought. But my underlying hope in corresponding with Augustine and Aquinas is to hear them speak to our own epoch. The two previous chapters' reading of their masterpieces sought to show how their strategy may guide the postmodern Christian. Here we further explore the lessons these spiritual and intellectual ancestors may offer us.

### The Historical Legacies
As we seek answers for our epoch, we do well first to ask, How did Augustine and Aquinas's works fare in their own epochs? The answer for both, it seems to me, is, Quite well; and not nearly well enough.

Both works undeniably served the church in significant ways. The pagan Romans' attempt to deconstruct Christianity as a harmful novelty was decisively defeated. Against the pagan assault, the church could rely on *City of God* to outdeconstruct the deconstructors. Furthermore, *City of God* certainly enabled the church to face life more confidently after the end of the Roman Empire. As discussed in chapter two, the postimperial church survived the Empire's collapse partly because its own learning and culture continued to thrive. *City of God* was upheld as an important example of distinctively Christian scholarship. As a result of Augustine's appropriation of classical learning, Christian culture did not give in to the impulse to purge itself of any and all nonbiblical influences, as some more fundamentalistic voices had advocated. Augustine paved the way for the monastic preservation of all learning in the so-called Dark Ages. Without *City of God,* the cultural inheritance of Christians—and of Western civilization in general—would have been greatly impoverished.

*Summa contra Gentiles* similarly emboldened medieval Christians to declaw Aristotle and domesticate his thinking within their own worldview. A full-scale purge of Aristotle never took place, even though the forces for such an intellectual pogrom were certainly present.[1]

Consequently, within a few centuries the church became the acknowledged sponsor of what we now call Western science. Without Aquinas it is conceivable that the Western church could have continued to perceive sensory-based experimentation, rational processes and other Aristotelian methods as hostile forces to keep at bay. Our historical inheritance could have included isolationist periods akin to the Middle Kingdom eras of China or the closed-door period of Tokugawa Japan. While the Enlightenment eventually pitted scientific learning against Christianity, the conflict might have happened earlier and in more irreconcilable ways had it not been for Aquinas. Finally, in works like *Summa contra Gentiles,* Aquinas ensured that philosophy could operate with and under Christian theology.[2] After completing the last volume of *SCG,* Aquinas proceeded to vanquish Siger of Brabant decisively in debate. The latter's separatist vision of faith and reason would not be exhumed until centuries later.

Yet despite all these contributions by *City of God* and *Summa contra Gentiles,* a deep ambivalence remains about their legacies. In some significant ways their underlying spirit and strategy were not extended to

---

[1]In fact, for a short time after Aquinas's death, conservative forces in the church continued to seek to ban Aristotle and even Aquinas. See Pegis, introduction to *SCG* 1, p. 22.

[2]See Étienne Gilson, *The Spirit of Mediaeval Philosophy* (Notre Dame, Ind.: University of Notre Dame Press, 1991), pp. 383-426.

subsequent generations. Both were sadly misappropriated by their descendants.

Augustine wrote *City of God* with more challengers than just the pagan Romans in mind. His metanarrative net was theoretically cast over all history to the ends of the earth and sought to capture all nonbelievers in its wake. He was keenly aware of the barbarian challenge that still needed to be engaged with the gospel. But after the pagan Roman challenger passed into antiquity, Augustine's descendants did not look very far beyond the borders of the former Empire. For several centuries after Augustine, precious few attempts were made to enter the barbarian world, much less reinterpret and incorporate it within the gospel.[3]

*City of God* was intended to help the church captivate Roman society, not embrace its prejudices. Robert Markus has documented how the post-Augustinian church, for all its praise of *City of God* as a classic, missed Augustine's underlying warning against conflating the City of God with earthly power. After the collapse of Rome the church remade itself as the sacred version of the Empire. Christianity so thoroughly shaped and dominated society that it ignored any other challenger—especially since its neglect of the barbarian world automatically excluded the most obvious potential challenger. When it finally got around to evangelizing the barbarian tribes, it sought to obliterate their stories by Christianizing them. To become a Christian, one was supposed to abandon one's barbarian world and adopt wholesale a particular, semi-Roman culture. For example, the church—grasping the integral relationship between language and culture—insisted that barbarian converts had to exchange their native tongue for Latin in order to comprehend the church's rites. The totalizing spirit of Rome captured the church as much as vice versa.[4]

It is tragic that a distinctively prophetic work like *City of God* could be simply enclosed by this spirit of the age. *City of God*, which itself so carefully acknowledged its challengers' culture, was often merely used to prove the uselessness of any other culture. Because the true spirit and

---

[3]Robert Markus, *Christianity in the Roman World* (London: Thames and Hudson, 1974), pp. 141-48.

[4]For this general perspective I am indebted to Robert Markus, *Saeculum* (London: Cambridge University Press, 1970), p. 163.

strategy of *City of God* did not take root, Aquinas had to inherit the epochal story of the Only City, a story that was too self-enclosed and ill-equipped to face the new challenge of Islam.

A parallel fate befell the legacy of Thomas Aquinas. The genius of Aquinas's philosophy was fairly quickly recognized and spawned an entire school of descendants. Thomistic scholasticism came to occupy an important place in Catholic thought. Unfortunately, many of Aquinas's followers inherited his genre but misplaced his underlying strategy. Fourteenth- and fifteenth-century scholasticism took Aquinas's technical categories, precise style of logic and use of Aristotle but turned inward with them. The school became engrossed in debates that only mattered internally to the Christian story, and even then the topics—like the infamous "how many angels can fit on the tip of a pin?" debate—hardly mattered much. Lost in such insular squabbles was the church's mission to unbelievers.

Scholasticism's use of reason and philosophy became so arid that it reopened the fissures that threatened Aquinas's day. In the Reformation, Luther would so recoil against scholasticism's hyper-rationality that according to legend he publicly burned Aquinas's works. Whether the legend is true or not, Luther certainly presented a version of the gospel that at least carried the seeds of pitting faith against reason and the Bible against philosophy. For example, in his *Disputation Against Scholastic Theology*, a crucial document published at the outset of the Reformation, Luther categorically declared: "Briefly, the whole Aristotle is to theology as darkness is to light."[5] Many of Luther's followers would embrace this divisive spirit of the age and sunder the very unities Aquinas had laboriously sought to preserve in *Summa contra Gentiles*.

Lost in both the scholastic misappropriation and Protestant rejection of Aquinas was the epochal challenge that had triggered *Summa contra Gentiles* in the first place. Aquinas remains the "great but lonely" exception in Christian responses to Islam. Little work was done to extend his effort to capture Islamic thought or even just to adapt *SCG* into a more

---

[5]Thesis 50 in Martin Luther, "Disputation Against Scholastic Theology," *Martin Luther's Basic Theological Writings*, ed. Timothy Lull (Minneapolis: Fortress, 1989), p. 16.

widely accessible form.[6] The Crusades would run their bloody course for another century, and the ensuing Reformation would ignore Islam. Missions to the Islamic lands would remain at low levels—a sad condition that also marks our epoch.[7]

It seems to me that the legacies of *City of God* and *Summa contra Gentiles* offer at least one clear lesson about how we ought to relate to such ancestral texts. We certainly need the wisdom of forebears like Augustine and Aquinas. But they also need us. These works originally arose in the demanding climate of mission, and to enclose them within a totalizing context is to transplant them out of their native enviornment. They fall stagnant and flat. To recover their lively and angular perspectives, each generation of readers must open these texts to the brisk air of mission in their own epoch.

In our current epoch there exists real danger that we might misplace their legacies altogether. In my undergraduate years at Harvard, the college offered only one course that included *City of God* on the reading list, and that course was only sporadically offered. As far as I can tell, no course examined *Summa contra Gentiles;* I had never even heard of the book until long after I graduated. While that may say more about my education than about anything else, the reality is that the average Protestant seminary student can graduate without ever having to read either of these monumental works.

When these works are examined, they suffer the fate of many books that bear the dusty label "Christian classics." The reader flips through *City of God* or *Summa contra Gentiles*, skipping Augustine's seemingly irrelevant discussions of Varro or Aquinas's abstract distinctions on the "eternity of the world" in order to find the classic quotes or obviously "relevant" sections. Publishers have reflected this demand for sound bites by producing various abridged versions of these works. One such

---

[6]Ramon Lull, one of the greatest missionaries to Islam, would praise Aquinas's work. But apart from such testimonials, there seems to have been little sustained effort to translate Aquinas's thought to the mission field. See James Waltz, "Muhammad and the Muslims in St. Thomas Aquinas," *The Muslim World* 66 (April 1976): 93.

[7]See Benjamin Z. Kedar, *Crusade and Mission* (Princeton, N.J.: Princeton University Press, 1984), pp. 160.

version carries the following introduction by a noted scholar:

> Many, perhaps most, readers never finish reading the *City of God* in its
> original form. It is a very long work. . . . The digressions in the *City of God*
> are often of great length. Finally, there are in this work very detailed
> accounts of ancient history, of Biblical events, of the teachings of Greek
> and Roman mythology, and of contemporary incidents *of no great impor-*
> *tance today. Most of this digressive material is omitted in the present edi-*
> *tion.*[8]

But when one omits such digressive material which the editor assumes
possesses "no great importance today," one misses the real relevance of
the whole work: its brilliant strategy and spirit. Reading the sound-bite
sections is better than nothing, but it is akin to glancing only at the last
moves of an epic Fischer-Spassky chess match or only bothering with the
most memorable lines of a Greek tragedy. One misses the whole story that
makes those quotations important in the first place.

Of course, the fault does not lie with either readers or publishers of
abridged versions of Augustine and Aquinas. Without assistance, the general reader cannot follow the context, spirit and strategy that animate
these works. Fostering a living correspondence between today's reader
and these ancient authors is precisely the responsibility of the church's
scholars.

Church historians bear particular responsibility for the impoverished
legacies of these two works. General readers have been reduced to
scrounging for sound-bite pieces partly because scholars themselves have
subjected these works to microscopic analysis. Smaller and smaller sections of these texts take up more and more academic attention. The rich
unity of these works has been fractured into narrow topics to be studied
within compartmentalized subfields. *City of God* and *Summa contra*
*Gentiles* are massively sturdy works, and they bear up reasonably well
under this scrutiny; but in the process their most winsome qualities are

---

[8]Vernon C. Bourke, introduction to Augustine, *City of God*, abridg. Vernon C. Bourke (New
York: Doubleday, 1958), pp. 10-11, emphasis mine. It is interesting to note that Aquinas's
more famous work, *Summa Theologica*, also was "dismembered by medieval copyists" after
his death. See Alasdair MacIntyre, *Three Rival Versions of Moral Enquiry* (Notre Dame,
Ind.: University of Notre Dame Press, 1990), p. 163.

lost to the wider church. These works are epics, and epics demand to be unleashed and retold, not sliced up and reduced.

The academic treatment of these two texts has followed a general retreat by the church history discipline. Like other Christian scholars, church historians have withdrawn into developing the technical expertise on narrowly defined subjects that secular academia so prizes. One symptom of this narrow retreat is the notable lack of comparative works in church history. Works that reflect a range of historical vision seem to be drowned by a plethora of detailed monographs and specialized studies. While specialized research certainly can be very helpful, it fails to serve the church unless it can be enlisted into a wider and more important mission.

This mission is suggested in really wonderful epics like the Lord of the Rings trilogy or the Chronicles of Narnia. In those tales there inevitably comes some moment when our heroes feel overwhelmed and unequipped as they face some daunting challenge. Our heroes can move forward only by encountering some treasure from the past. It might be a cache of ancient weapons: swords and amulets that our heroes need to relearn how to wield. Almost always, those old weapons and tactics turn out to be the only way to overcome the current obstacle. Or the treasure may be a tale of ancient battles—a grand story that our heroes retell. And almost always that story emboldens them to face anew the challenge before them.

Church historians are keepers of such treasures. We preserve ancient strategies, swords and songs. We repair and compare them. We treasure them, not to inspect them with ever more minute attention, but to ready them for the day when they will be needed again. We church historians need to be willing to restore and retell grand stories for our day. For we must give the church stories compelling enough to captivate its challengers. Lose the epic, and you risk losing the epoch.

## Obeying Christ in Our Rhetorical Strategy

But we do not wage war according to human standards; for the weapons of our warfare are not merely human, but they have divine power to destroy strongholds. We destroy arguments and every proud obstacle raised up

against the knowledge of God, and we take every thought captive to obey
Christ. (2 Cor 10:3-5)

My opening chapter defined an epochal challenge as a particularly
unsettling conflict of worldviews. This conflict between Christians and
their opponents cannot be resolved by appeals to conventions inherited
from the previous epoch, and thus both sides are locked in an argument
where less and less can actually be said. Such a state intensifies the
human temptation to abandon words and instead wage war. Thus if the
Christian wishes to avoid simply resorting to physical, political or even
cultural coercion, she will need a rhetorical strategy for the new epoch.

This need has recurred in the history of the church. The apostle Paul
himself corresponded with the Corinthian church about temptations to
"wage war according to human standards" when encountering the
"strongholds" of rival worldviews. The main goal of this book has been to
foster a correspondence with Augustine and Aquinas that reveals their
rhetorical strategy as a possible alternative response for our own epoch.
Borrowing Paul's terms in 2 Corinthians 10, I have titled this rhetorical
strategy "taking every thought captive." But another question naturally
arises: does the "taking every thought captive" strategy actually empower
Christians today to engage with their postmodern challengers?

If this question were posed to the postmodern challenger, he or she
likely would dismiss the strategy out of hand. The challenger might argue,
"Doesn't the very title of the strategy, 'Taking Every Thought Captive,'
reveal the recurrent violence and arrogance of Christianity?"

A critic like my Native American friend Jake would not even need to
resort to a very sophisticated deconstruction of the three stages of
"enter," "retell" and "capture" to accuse: "Ah, here again is the Christian
impulse to invade, violate and imprison opponents like my tribal ancestors!"

And a relativist like the student Alex would argue that the Christian's
haughty claim to encompass "every thought" disguises how all thoughts—
including Christian thought—are themselves actually subject to an epistemology of radical doubt.

For such postmodern challengers, "taking every thought captive" might appear to confirm the worst of Christianity: a history of marginalizing the other and an arrogance in claiming total certitude. At least initially, this strategy hardly seems like the recipe for successfully persuading postmodern opponents.

Such initial reactions need to be taken seriously. Nevertheless, the likely response of any human being is never the starting or ending point for evaluating the rhetorical strategy of a Christian. It should be obvious to evangelists with any experience that no rhetorical strategy can guarantee a favorable response. Among the pagans and Muslims who were exposed to the brilliance of *City of God* and *Summa contra Gentiles*, multitudes undoubtedly continued to reject the gospel. The apostle Paul himself wrote to the Corinthians in an earlier letter: "But we proclaim Christ crucified, a stumbling block to Jews and foolishness to Gentiles" (1 Cor 1:23).

Instead of being assured a favorable response we are instructed to faithfully "proclaim Christ crucified." In 2 Corinthians 10, Paul repeats his belief that only speech that witnesses to Christ crucified possesses divine power to engage with rivals. Any other approach, he seems to suggest, leads to "war according to human standards." Thus in any epoch, but especially in our conflict-ridden age, our rhetorical strategy must obey Christ.

"Obeying Christ" in passages like 2 Corinthians 10 (and countless others in Scripture) certainly means that Jesus Christ, that unique person who was crucified and raised from the dead, must stand as the actual content of all our rhetoric. No story or strategy can ultimately save our world; only this Person can. So *what* we say must always lead back to the *who* of Jesus Christ.

But *how* we speak—what I have throughout this book called "rhetorical strategy"—must also bear faithful witness to Christ. Among Christian thinkers engaging with postmodern unbelief, the theological evaluation of rhetorical strategy has generally been overshadowed by the evaluation of content. But Paul himself frequently felt it necessary to justify his own manner of speaking. Especially in his relationship with the Corinthian church, Paul defends his rhetorical strategy on christological grounds. For example, he argues that the Corinthians' belief that Paul's "speaking amounts to nothing" (2 Cor 10:10 NIV) is erroneous, for his manner of speech is modeled by the Lord himself (2 Cor 10:8). Similarly, Paul demonstrates that his preaching style, with all its "weakness and fear, and with much trembling" (1 Cor 2:3 NIV), follows the christological pattern of God's choosing "what is foolish in the world" (1 Cor 1:27).

Thus the evaluative questions are these: Does the rhetorical strategy pursued by Augustine and Aquinas follow a christological model? And correspondingly, will our own way of speaking to the postmodern truly obey Christ?

These questions again highlight the pressing need for Christian academics to break out of narrow disciplinary confines, for the answer requires the combined efforts of scholars in Christology, church history and homiletics-apologetics. Or to put it in less technical terms, the questions again demonstrate the wider mission shared by Christian theologians, historians and preachers alike.

While this section mainly aims to stimulate a further cross-disciplinary conversation, I suggest that the "taking every thought captive" strategy does witness faithfully to the church's historical consensus on the person and work of Christ. That is, the *how* of this strategy points to the *who* of Christ. Specifically, the three stages of enter, retell and capture serve as analogies corresponding with the classic doctrines of Christ's incarnation, recapitulation and atonement.

*The incarnation.* Early church history is filled with seemingly arcane disputes about the exact nature of the incarnation. The early church fathers labored so hard because they recognized the high stakes involved. At issue is exactly how God entered human existence in the person of Christ. Against heresies like Docetism or Apollinarianism the church fathers insisted that Christ fully adopted all the terms of humanity. The great fourth-century preacher John Chrysostom loved to speak of Christ's *kenosis:* his voluntary acceptance of human limitations.[9] Thinkers like Athanasius and Gregory Nazianzen further clarified how Christ could completely inhabit humanity without losing his distinctive nature as

---

[9]John Chrysostom, *Homilies on Philippians* 6, in Nicene and Post-Nicene Fathers of the Christian Church (hereafter NPNF), ed. H. Wace and P. Schaff (New York: Christian, 1887-1900), 2/13, pp. 206-12.

God.[10] The Fourth Ecumenical Council of Chalcedon summarized this union as "without confusion or change."

Augustine and Aquinas both enter their challengers' stories along this incarnational pattern. Both fully adopt the challengers' terms and authorities as their own. Both take great pains to restrict themselves initially to the authoritative texts of their opponents. Yet they enter the pagan and Islamic stories still retaining their distinctive Christian identities. They refuse to give in to some confusing syncretism or an intellectual appeasement that would change the essence of the gospel.

In the voluntary decision to initially limit themselves to their opponents' terms, I believe neither was simply motivated by a pragmatic desire to win the argument by any means necessary. It is important to remember that in both of their epochs, military and intellectual versions of the crusade were viable options. For the vast majority of Christians in their respective epochs, requiring challengers to surrender their weapons *and* story seemed like a perfectly reasonable prerequisite for any meeting. But Augustine and Aquinas issue no such demands. Both bear the intellectual costs involved in establishing genuine communication across the battle lines.

This desire for real communication reflects a persistent theme in the Fathers' reflection on the incarnation. Tertullian, who preceded Augustine as the definitive voice of early African Christianity, emphasized how the incarnation communicates God's true character, especially his divine empathy with a humanity which was so "other."[11] The early councils understood that this empathy incarnated in Christ was crucial to reconciling the conflict between God and humanity. Thomas Oden summarizes the patristic position: "The mediator between God and humanity would have to be nothing less than God and nothing less than fully human, otherwise this mediatorship would have been impossible, for how can one mediate in a conflict in which one has no capacity to empathize with one or the other side?"[12]

---

[10]Athanasius *On the Incarnation of the Word* 14-15, in NPNF 2/14:43-44. Gregory Nazianzen *Orations* 29.19, in NPNF 2/7:308.

[11]Tertullian *Apology* 2, in Ante-Nicene Fathers (hereafter ANF), ed. A. Roberts and J. Don aldson (Grand Rapids, Mich.: Eerdmans, 1979).

[12]Thomas Oden, *The Word of Life* (New York: HarperCollins, 1989), p. 119.

Augustine's and Aquinas's writings also repeatedly depict the incarnation in terms of a reconciling mediator.[13] It seems reasonable to assume that as they sought a rhetorical strategy to engage with their challengers, their minds would have turned to Christ the Mediator of all epochs. Just as Christ had to fully adopt the human story in the conflict between God and humanity, so Augustine and Aquinas had to fully adopt their challengers' stories in their particular epochal conflicts.

*Recapitulation.* In the "taking every thought captive" strategy, entering the challengers' story is closely related to retelling the story. Augustine and Aquinas rework the opposing stories from the inside. Neither resorts to authorities external to the challengers' world. Each offers a retelling of his challengers' story that purports to be more authentic by the challengers' own standards. In a very real sense they seek to be even more truly pagan or Aristotelian than their Roman or Islamic counterparts.

This retelling corresponds to the christological doctrine that bears the suggestive title "recapitulation." Reflecting on biblical passages like Ephesians 1:10, Tertullian, Athanasius, Justin Martyr and others taught that Christ embraced all of humanity and "reheaded" the human race in the right direction. Irenaeus especially emphasized how "God recapitulated in Himself the ancient formation of man, that he might kill sin, deprive death of its power and vivify man."[14] That God did not reorder humanity by fiat or resort to some other external force was so central to the early fathers that they formulated the classic patristic dictum "That which has not been assumed has not been healed." Christ reworked the human condition from within the human story and thus becomes the One True Human.

Significantly, this reworking of humanity from within could be accomplished only by Christ, the Son of God who had entered humanity from outside. Left to itself, humanity could never have fully achieved its true state. It is by virtue of his divinity—his very otherness—that Christ

---

[13]See *COG* 9:15, p. 359, and *COG* 19.9, p. 864; also Augustine *Sermon on New Testament Lessons* 47, in NPNF 1/6:412. For Aquinas, see *Summa Theologica* (New York: Benziger, 1947), 3.Q26.1 (2:2158).

[14]Irenaeus *Against Heresies* 3.18.7, in ANF 1:448

becomes fully human and in himself remakes us as fully human.

In analogous fashion it is by virtue of their Christian perspective that Augustine and Aquinas are able to retell their challengers' stories. While at this second stage they still refrain from explicitly bringing in the gospel, they are implicitly arguing that they—as ones who have entered the rival story from outside—can accomplish what those who dwell solely within the rival story cannot. Only they can name the key internal flaws; only they can correctly interpret the deepest intentions of the main characters.

It is as if Augustine and Aquinas are editors listening intently to a struggling novelist read a first draft. The novel's characters are not adequately developed; but in a phenomenon familiar to any writer, the novelist has been immersed for too long in this story to be able to name the problems. Because the editors possess a wider perspective from reading other stories and in fact from knowing the Best Story Ever (to stretch this analogy to its breaking point!), they can say, "What this character really should do at this point in plot is *this* . . ." And because the editors have already sympathetically entered the narrative world of the novelist, their retellings are faithful to the novelist's deepest (perhaps even unconscious) intentions, such that the writer exclaims, "Yes, of course!"

What this analogy and the retelling stage of "taking every thought captive" are trying to suggest is one of the great mysteries in the recapitulation: that only the wholly Other can tell me who I truly am. This mystery of Christ targets a key stronghold of postmoderns. Postmodern intellectuals claim to have discovered the wisdom that relationship with another must inevitably lead to the violation of the self. In their historical, sociological and psychological stories, postmodern intellectuals seek to recount how the lines drawn between "other" and "self" are inevitably battle lines. Thus they assert that a Christ and a Christianity that seek to rework other stories must repeat this violent pattern.

We need not bow to this verdict of the "wise" and lapse into silence. For Aquinas especially recognized that Christ's strategy differed profoundly from the fallen human pattern of coercion and violence. In book 3, chapter 88 of *Summa contra Gentiles* he accepts Aristotle's definition of violence as an external agent exerting unnatural influence. Because

God is intimately and naturally present within humanity, Aquinas argues, "God alone can move the will in the fashion of an agent, without violence."[15] Several chapters later Aquinas repeatedly demonstrates that "God by His help does not force men to right action." In Christ, God rejects any coercion to correct humanity. Instead God offers himself in Christ as a free gift of grace. This grace is the antithesis of violence, for this gift restores an object to its true, natural state. God's grace, according to Aquinas's famous dictum, "does not destroy nature but perfects it."[16]

Against the backdrop of the crusades, Aquinas clearly perceived the implications of this Christology for rhetorical strategy. From the way God works, Aquinas draws the following conclusion: "So, no created substance can move the will except by means of a good which is understood. Now, this is done by showing it that something is a good thing to do: this is the act of persuading. Therefore, no created substance can act on the will, or be the cause of our act of choice, except in the way of a persuading agent."[17]

The hundreds of chapters of *Summa contra Gentiles* represent Aquinas's efforts to persuade Islam not by the sword but by "showing it that something is a good thing to do." He engages in the act of persuading his challengers such that the Aristotelian story is not destroyed but reworked to its truly intended state.

*The atonement.* While Jesus Christ's recapitulation of humanity is not a violent act on his part, his action does reveal violence on humanity's part. In many of the stories Jesus tells, like the parable of the tenants and the vineyard (Mk 12:1-8), he recounts humanity's forceful and brutal resistance to God. More important, the gospel accounts of Jesus' own trial and crucifixion starkly present the twin human flaws that drive this violence: pride and insistence on self-sufficiency.

Jesus' own life story exposed the violent pride of his persecutors. As the ancient Russian Catechism puts it, "The elders of the Jews and the scribes hated him, because he rebuked their false doctrine and evil lives, and envied him, because the people, which heard him teach and saw his miracles, esteemed him more than them; and hence they falsely accused

---

[15]*SCG* 3.88.6, p. 35 (part 2).
[16]SCG 3.148.2, p. 226 (part 2).
[17]*SCG* 3.88.2, p. 33 (part 2).

him, and condemned him to death."[18] And in the killing of Jesus, human epistemological inadequacy was laid bare before all. This is why, according to Athanasius, the death of Christ could not be a private death due to natural causes but had to take the form of a public execution intentionally carried out by human beings. The crucifixion displayed the human failure to know the highest truth, to recognize the very face of God.[19] One of the many ironies of the atonement is that in allowing himself to be stripped naked, Christ exposed fallen humanity; in giving himself up to captivity, he captured the human tragedy.

Not surprisingly, Augustine and Aquinas craft their metanarratives with these twin human flaws in mind. Augustine's *City of God* unveils the pride lurking underneath every human empire; Aquinas's *Summa contra Gentiles* demonstrates the insufficiency of all human reason. And like the atonement, their "capture" stage makes clear that these flaws ultimately drive the conflict between the gospel and the challenger's story. Other reasons for sustaining the conflict are stripped away. If the Christian storyteller has truly "entered," then challengers cannot claim the Christian is merely shouting incomprehensible foreign terms; if the Christian has truly "retold," then challengers cannot claim their story is misunderstood by the Christian. Instead, the true reason for rejection is "captured": the deep-rooted human temptation to star in one's own self-sufficient story.

At this stage Christians must understand for themselves—and communicate to challengers as much as they are willing to listen—that this sort of capture radically differs from the "human standards of warfare." It is not as if the Christian side wins mastery, taking the challengers as slaves or triumphantly seizing them as prisoners. For one thing, *all* of humanity is captured by the gospel metanarrative. The atonement narratives show Jesus' followers with the same flaws as their opponents: Peter arrogantly boasts that he will be the star disciple, and the other disciples cannot rationally deduce the true identity of Jesus. Analogously, Augustine and Aquinas depict pride and rational insufficiency as encompassing not just Rome or Islam but also those who call themselves Christians.

---

[18]The Russian Catechism, in *Creeds of Christendom*, ed. Phillip Schaff (New York: Harper, 1919), 1:474.

[19]Athanasius *Incarnation of the Word* 21-25, in NPNF 2/4:47-49.

More important, this rhetorical capture does not just reveal human flaws but actually resolves them. The capture stage bears witness to the atonement, the event that N. T. Wright has called "the victory of God."[20] And this divine victory is utterly unlike any human military triumph. The nature of God's maneuvers in the atonement is one of the most profound mysteries of the gospel and defies easy diagramming. Reflecting on patristic thought, Calvin described the atonement as the "wonderful exchange." Contemporary theologians like Thomas Torrance have called it "the double movement of Christ." This exchange and movement is summarized as "Christ ministering the things of God to us, and ours to God."[21]

In the atonement Christ brings to us God's own resolution of the tragic tension of sin. In the atonement Jesus Christ offers every "stuck" human story a way forward. In Christ our tragic flaws of pride and self-sufficiency are offered up to God in exchange for Christ's own humility and dependence on the Father. Therefore in Christ every human being and human story can be completed by being taken into a wider, more compelling and more experiential relationship with God and his story.

Church tradition from the apostle Paul onward has recognized that Christ's completion of the human story represents the climax of divine love. Bishop Christoph Schönborn, principal editor of the current catechism of the Catholic Church, summarizes this act in terms that are suggestive for our discussion: "In Christ, the final purpose of creation has been revealed: the union of humanity and divinity in a paradoxical conquest. . . . This conquest, which leads human nature to its ultimate perfection, is called *love*."[22]

The strategy of "capture" that Augustine and Aquinas pursue testifies to this conquest of love. Even when exposing their opponents' tragic flaws, they evidence great empathy and even affection. Each welcomes

---

[20]N. T. Wright, *Jesus and the Victory of God* (Minneapolis: Fortress, 1996), p. 610. For more on the doctrine of the "wonderful exchange," see Martin Luther, *Commentary on Galatians* (London: James Clarke, 1953), pp. 168-71; and John Calvin, *Institutes of the Christian Religion* (Grand Rapids, Mich.: Eerdmans, 1949), 2.12.2.

[21]Oden, *Word of Life*, p. 370, and Thomas F. Torrance, *The Mediation of Christ* (Grand Rapids, Mich.: Eerdmans, 1984), p. 73.

[22]Christoph Schönborn, *God's Human Face* (San Francisco: Ignatius, 1994), p. 124

the good desires found in the challengers' story and actually seeks to intensify those hungers. And Augustine and Aquinas so indwell the pagan and Aristotelian narratives that they know them inside and out; they can precisely point to the internal tensions that the gospel metanarrative must resolve. Thus each masters his opponent not as a tyrant oppresses a slave but as an artisan grasps all the features of a work of art. They capture the challenger not as a soldier seizes a prisoner but as a suitor captivates his beloved's heart.

In the atonement this conquest of love also achieves the other movement of the wonderful exchange: bringing humanity to God. Oden summarizes the classic Christian consensus that "there is now a person in the Trinity in whom human experience has become indissolubly united with the eternal God." That Christ ascended to heaven with a body which still bore the marks of humanity (even the marks of a human crucifixion) testifies to how fully Christ brings the human story into God's presence.[23] While God did not need humanity—this union "is not a result of the inadequacy of divine power," as Aquinas puts it—God has out of his love brought humanity into a place of lasting significance.[24] Thus Christ's conquest does not obliterate human beings but actually accords them genuine participation in the divine. This is why near the end of the *City of God* Augustine goes out of his way to emphasize that human attributes will still thrive in the eternal metanarrative of life with God.[25] Yes there is a real human surrender involved, but it is only postmodernism's tragic attachment to pride and self-sufficiency that insists all surrender is obliteration and coercion. There is a self-surrender that is love: the love of Christ that unites humanity to God.

In analogous fashion Augustine and Aquinas both seek to rhetorically capture their challengers. Both clearly believe that in principle the gospel is a self-sufficient metanarrative. In his classic treatise on Christian education, *De doctrina christiana,* Augustine rejects the notion that every Christian must learn the Roman classics. Similarly, in his opening to *Summa contra Gentiles* Aquinas acknowledges that Christian salvation

---

[23]Oden, *Word of Life*, p. 468.
[24]*SCG* 3.70.7, p. 237 (part 1).
[25]*COG* 22.4-5, pp. 1026-29; *COG* 22.15-21, pp. 1055-64

does not depend on philosophical discourse, much less on reading challenging thinkers like Aristotle.[26] Yet both take great pains voluntarily to give the pagan and Aristotelian narratives a real role in their versions of the gospel metanarrative. In fact, several pagan works would otherwise have completely vanished, obliterated from our consciousness like so many other ancient texts in history. Some of Marcus Varro's texts, for instance, come to us today only because Augustine gave them a place in *City of God.* Indeed, *City of God* and *Summa contra Gentiles* have been regarded as Christian classics for so long that it is easy to forget how these works are inextricably intertwined with their challengers. If all references to Roman authors and Islamic philosophers were suddenly stripped from *City of God* and *Summa contra Gentiles*, these books would be unrecognizable. Again, as emphasized above in the discussion of the incarnation, both works are presenting the gospel "without confusion." Yet each book also bears the marks of an indissoluble union with its particular challengers. In capturing challengers, each book has also given itself to the challengers.

The peculiar nature of this "conquest of love" gives rise to an important—but difficult—set of questions for all who would attempt the "taking every thought captive" strategy. Christian storytellers must ask themselves whether they are timidly shying away from full conquest. Are we telling stories that actually confront human pride and self-sufficiency, those age-old enemies of all true love and especially divine love? Postmodernism is right to call us back to the importance of narrative, but our epoch also tempts us to hide behind deceptive banners such as *tolerance* and *diversity* and to tell the wrong stories. Will we simply repeat stories that legitimate the tragic human resistance to God, or will we boldly proclaim the gospel, the only story that is God's own invitation to surrender our incomplete selves to his all-completing love?

At the same time, Christian storytellers must examine whether they are imperialistically pursuing the wrong conquest. Does the "capturing" metanarrative offer an ongoing significance to the challengers' narrative?

---

[26]Augustine, *De doctrina christiana*, ed. D. W. Robertson (New York: Bobbs Merrill, 1958), 2.13; *SCG* 1.4, pp. 66-68.

Does our particular version of the Christian metanarrative remain the gospel "without confusion" yet allow itself to be so taken by challengers that they are united to each other in a lasting way? In other words, are our challengers crushed into obliteration or truly embraced by the eternal metanarrative of God's love?

This sort of engagement is not easy. More than brilliant intellects and words must be deployed. Such weapons may be helpful and even necessary to Christians, but they have been regularly wielded also by those bearing the standards of human warfare. The unique "divine power to demolish strongholds" is instead borne by the cross. At the cross Jesus Christ defeated all rivals not by force, not by intellect, not even by uttered rhetoric. At the cross Jesus Christ conquered with his suffering love. In Christ crucified, God so loved humanity that he bore all the painful ways the human tragedy has been imprisoned by pride and self-sufficiency, violence and resistance. He willingly submitted to this captivity. And thus he accomplished the startling maneuver of the atonement: in a most wonderful exchange of prisoners, the captive One set us free. By suffering our captivity while still embracing God's love, he truly defeated every thought that sets itself against the knowledge of God's love.

The question of how our rhetorical strategy can testify to Christ's conquest of love is a daunting one. For the atonement seems to suggest that ultimately what will speak most loudly is our willingness to suffer with and for our challengers. I am not sure I know what it means to speak as one who so loves the challenger before me. I confess I have had all too few experiences of doing so. Yet so befriending my challengers that their pain becomes mine must certainly affect the timbre of my voice, the tone of my rhetoric.

"Taking every thought captive" seeks to embody rhetorically Christ's own strategy of transformative love. The strategy attempts to rescue the challengers' story from incompletion and bring it to its true and best purpose. It aims to redeem the engagement from intractable conflict to conquering love. And it seeks to transform challengers from enemies to the beloved of God.

In the process our challengers are not the only ones being transformed. Indeed, we who pursue this strategy cannot demand that our challengers bear the brunt of this transformation. We must pay the costs. We must take the necessary pains to establish a common ground; we must labor to offer persuasive corrections; we must share in their suffering. In short, we mirror the crucified Christ. As we rhetorically reflect Christ, we spiritually undergo what the apostle Paul described to the Corinthians: "Seeing the glory of the Lord as though reflected in a mirror, [we] are being transformed into the same image from one degree of glory to another; for this comes from the Lord, the Spirit" (2 Cor 3:18).

### Applying the Strategy Today

If my attempt to establish a correspondence between rhetorical strategy and classical Christology is persuasive, then "taking every thought captive" possesses the potential to convey divine power to the strongholds of the postmodern epoch. What specific steps might realize this potential is a huge topic and deserves further attention elsewhere and by others. In fact, the enter, retell and capture steps could organize and empower a distinctly Christian program of scholarship. Let us consider some possible avenues such a program could take.

*Entering new media.* How we enter the postmodern story involves the crucial question of genre. Augustine composed a historical treatise and Aquinas employed philosophical reasoning because each represented the most incarnational form of communication for his epoch. Today, the most common genre of discourse the church utilizes is inherited from previous epochs: the "lecture," or in more Christian terms, the "sermon." Alasdair MacIntyre points out that the effectiveness of this genre rests on conditions that reigned up through modernity but no longer rule our epoch. For example, the lecture assumes assent to the authority of the speaker as "expert" and widespread agreement on the rules of truth seeking.

In my own experience of preaching to college students, I have noticed that compared to even ten years ago there exists a greater suspicion of the speaker and a weaker sense of biblical authority even among those who identify themselves as Christians. For the nonbeliever especially, the sort of sermon commonly preached in church tends to assume what it actually needs to establish. How can the sermon genre be adapted to the postmodern audience? Sermons that hope to captivate the imagination of postmoderns will rely on the narrative genre. This will require a rethinking of the art of preaching such that narrative categories replace the current tendency to present three main points abstracted from Scripture.[27]

Training in narrative preaching does not mean simply teaching preachers to tell funnier anecdotes or share more personal details of their lives (although both could be helpful!). It is all too tempting to tell the wrong stories, narratives that merely reinforce our desire to be our own star and legitimate our own experiences. The story needed is the gospel itself, and the preachers required are ones who can make *this* story come alive for us.

While preaching will always play an important role in the church, entering the postmodern story will require exploring different genres and indeed altogether different media. The dawn of the postmodern epoch coincided with an enormous media revolution. In the past fifty years the image has rivaled and in many ways supplanted the word as the dominant form of communication. The average postmodern in the West now discourses in all sorts of new visual genres and media like sitcom television shows, websites and virtual reality video games.

But at the center of the culture stands cinema. Movies convey the stories of postmoderns in a way no other medium does. When I sit down with a table of college students at Harvard and ask them about their views on some historical event or philosophical position, some will give me polite, considered replies, and others will mutely shrug their shoulders. But when I ask what are their favorite movies and why, their eyes light up and almost everyone has something to say, often agreeing or disagreeing with each other quite passionately. Indeed, in our fractured and privatized society, viewing and talking about films together are some of the few public activities still thriving.

Entering our challengers' story will mean entering the movie theater with them. Yet Christian scholars have been surprisingly remiss in surveying this potential common ground. There does not exist any definitive theology of cinema that parallels Augustine's theology of history or

---

[27]See Richard Eslinger, *Narrative and Imagination: Preaching the Worlds That Shape Us* (Minneapolis: Fortress, 1995).

Aquinas's theology of philosophical reasoning. The overwhelming majority of theological forays into cinema that do exist simply analyze the themes and plots of specific movies.[28] While such books can be helpful, understanding various messages is not the same as grasping the medium. This partly explains why none of these books have lasted as definitive works: they are too bound to specific movies that happened to be popular at the time of writing and to relatively transient cultural messages. Theologians still have not measured the unique dimensions of cinema as medium.

Numerous unaddressed questions confront the cinematically attuned Christian. What would it mean for Christians to adopt the visual terms and standards of Hollywood? Where is authority located in a given viewing experience? Do some cinematic genres offer more common ground than others? What happens to the gospel when it inhabits various aesthetic devices unique to cinema, like montage and multiple points of view? Or on a very obvious level, who is actually being projected when an actor pretending to be Christ enters the scene? Clearly, there are dangers facing the Christian as he or she enters the movie theater. Jacques Ellul, one of the few theologians who sought to analyze visual media, argued that the "realism" of such modern media intrinsically empties out the truth of the gospel. In fact, he claimed, true gospel rhetoric is impossible when incarnated in a medium like cinema which "humiliates" the word.[29]

Addressing such fundamental concerns will require renewing a correspondence with the proper ancestors. Epochal shifts in media should especially direct our attention to the Eastern Orthodox theologians of the icon. Western Christians, especially those influenced by the Reformation, have tended to be suspicious of Eastern iconography. While the Orthodox theology of the image is certainly open to critique, Protestants often make too facile a critique, ignoring the Orthodox tradition's history of intense

---

[28]For such examples see Robert Jewett, *Saint Paul at the Movies* (Louisville: Westminster John Knox, 1993); Bernard Brandon Scott, *Hollywood Dreams and Biblical Stories* (Minneapolis: Fortress, 1994); Margaret Miles, *Seeing and Believing: Religion and Values in the Movies* (Boston: Beacon, 1996).

[29]Jacques Ellul, *Humiliation of the Word*, trans. J. M. Hanks (Grand Rapids, Mich.: Eerdmans, 1985).

grappling with the question of how to faithfully enter visual media.

Again the act of "entering" the challengers' story must follow the christological pattern of the incarnation. Not surprisingly, in the iconoclasm controversy of the eighth century, when the iconographers were attacked for their choice of the paint medium and the portrait genre, Orthodox theologians like John of Damascus and Theodore the Studite centered their justification of icons on a "visual" theology of the incarnation. In the incarnation God emptied and humiliated himself into a visually "circumscribable" form.[30]

Even if Protestants come away from dialogue with such thinkers without fully accepting Orthodox iconographic practices, we can still gain much insight from this rich tradition of theological reflection on visual media. For instance, more contemporary Orthodox theologians like Paul Evdokimov and Pavel Florensky have developed christological perspectives on the spirituality involved in creating images and the aesthetics of proper viewership.[31]

Renewing this correspondence could also greatly benefit the iconographic tradition. During the century of cinema's ascendancy, the Orthodox Church has shown little to no interest in exploring the new medium. This may be due to the historical context of the Greek and Russian Orthodox traditions during the twentieth century. Both have been forced into a culturally defensive posture: the former in regard to Islam and the latter in response to communism. The result has been an increasingly self-enclosed body of thought, detached from the new challenges swirling in the wider society. Even an Orthodox theologian as conversant with modernity as Paul Evdokimov will hint that other media like classical architecture or Mozart's music can serve some of the same functions as a traditional icon, but will fail to deal with cinema at any length.[32] Like *City of God* and *Summa contra Gentiles*, the iconographical literature must be

---

[30]John of Damasucs, *On the Divine Images* (Crestwood, N.Y.: St. Vladimir's Seminary Press, 1977), p. 18. For more on the iconoclasm controversy, see Daniel J. Sahas, *Icon and Logos* (Toronto: University of Toronto Press, 1986).

[31]Pavel Florensky, *Iconostasis*, trans. by D. Sheehan and O. Andrejev (Crestwood, N.Y.: St. Vladimir's Seminary Press, 1996); see also Paul Phan, *Culture and Eschatology: The Iconographical Vision of Paul Evdokimov* (New York: Peter Lang, 1985).

[32]See Phan, *Culture and Eschatology*, p. 288.

opened up to new missiological imperatives if it is to remain a living
voice.

While great benefit could emerge from a conversation between the
theology of the icon and the medium of cinema, such conversation
appears sparse to nonexistent. Theologians who have written on cinema
instead suffer from acute historical short-sightedness. For instance, in
*Seeing and Believing* Margaret Miles chooses liberation and feminist
theologians as her main theological dialogue partners; she makes only a
passing and generalized reference to the theology of the icon.[33] Other
writers share this tendency, bringing the cinematic medium into conversation only with relatively contemporary thinkers like Martin Heidegger,
Harvey Cox or Paul Tillich.[34] Yet the theology of the icon deals far more
explicitly with images than Heidegger, Cox or any liberation and feminist
theologian ever does. Furthermore, iconography enjoys a far more
ancient intellectual tradition and a far more continuous religious practice
than does the thought of modern Protestant liberals like Tillich. The
Orthodox tradition and practice of icons have stood the test of numerous
challenges over the centuries. When faced with a challenge like a media
revolution, the church especially needs to correspond with its oldest
thinkers.

*Retelling the postmodern self.* The second stage of "taking every
thought captive" involves reworking the challengers' narrative by recourse
to some authority acknowledged by the challengers. Retelling the postmodern story is an especially complex task because this story is so much
about rejecting authoritative truth claims. The prime and only authority
in the story is the self. Thus an attempt to correct "from the inside" must
get inside the postmodern self. Christians must be prepared to tap into
the postmodern self's own experience of self.

Some contemporary scholars like Christopher Lasch, Robert Bellah
and Charles Taylor have already begun this project with great insight.

---

[33]See Miles, *Seeing and Believing*, pp. 187-89.
[34]For examples see Thomas M. Martin, *Images and the Imageless: A Study in Religious Consciousness and Film* (Lewisburg, Penn.: Bucknell University Press, 1991), pp. 48-49, 105-
9; Michael Bird, "Film as Hierophany," in *Religion in Film*, ed. John R. May and Michael
Bird (Knoxville: University of Tennessee Press, 1982), pp. 4-21.

Taking different angles, they have noted the constricted nature of an identity that rejects any narrative other than its own personal story.[35] In my ministry, I have found it very helpful to reinterpret commonly experienced symptoms of "the imploding self" back to a postmodern audience. Whenever possible, my strategy has been to heighten the postmodern's internal sense that something is tragically flawed: for example, her desperate need to worship objects and images even as she claims to be self-sufficient, or his enslavement to addictions even as he claims freedom from any other authority.

Many of these flaws stem from a central tension that traps the postmodern self. On the one hand, this self rejects the modern human being's confident self-image as a completely autonomous entity. The detached, objective observer is exposed as a fraudulent self-projection. But this self also clings to the suspicion that any relationship with someone different inevitably leads to some form of oppression and obliteration. Among students in my ministry, this internal contradiction is felt most intensely in their conflicting experiences of romance and sex. They are whipsawed back and forth from desperately wanting someone to "complete me" to fearing a loss of identity.

Correcting these conflicting internal understandings of self is crucial. The postmodern needs to be persuaded that there exists a way out of the imploding self if she or he is to be captivated by the metanarrative of a relationship with the divine Lover.

If providing an entire epoch with a reinterpretation of the self seems daunting, remember that the church has accomplished this once before in its history. When the early church entered the Hellenistic world, it confronted notions of personhood hostile to the gospel. Like many postmoderns, the Greeks conceived of self-identity as illusory and shifting: the main term for "person" was *prosopon*, a term also used for the mask Greek actors wore on stage. When the church sought to make doctrines like the incarnation and especially the Trinity intelligible,

[35]Christopher Lasch, *The Minimal Self* (New York: W. W. Norton, 1984); Robert Bellah et al., *Habits of the Heart: Individualism and Commitment in American Life* (Berkeley: University of California Press, 1985). See also Charles Taylor, *Sources of the Self: The Making of the Modern Identity* (Cambridge, Mass.: Harvard University Press, 1989).

Christian thinkers soon realized that they had to transform Greco-Roman categories of the self.

Augustine himself played an important role in this overall effort. His *On the Trinity* explored the way the human person was made in the image of the triune God, in the process depicting various triune relationships within the human self such as that of memory, understanding and will. These original insights eventually came to shape the West's understanding of human nature for centuries, and they still do today.

Eastern Christians especially labored over centuries to both enter and correct highly technical Greek terms for personhood like *hypostasis*, eventually redefining them for incorporation into the credal formulations of the gospel.

Today's Christian scholars undoubtedly need to enter psychology, anthropology, biology and the other sciences to correct distorted notions of personhood. But more than scientific descriptions, we need compelling stories that simply show what it means to be human. This is the realm of art, music and literature. In his *Confessions* Augustine created what was for his time a breathtakingly original piece of literature, a narration of how one discovers oneself as a true self. In the climactic book 10 of the *Confessions* he describes this process in the form of a passionate prayer: "Let me know you, for you are the God who knows me; let me recognize you as you have recognized me."[36] According to Charles Taylor, Augustine's depiction of "our dependence on God in the very intimacy of our presence to ourselves . . . [was] hallowed with immensely far-reaching consequences for the whole of Western culture."[37] A truly human story can transform an entire culture, readying it for the gospel.

*Capturing: Our version of the story.* The work of developing points of entry and correction must ultimately lead to the capture of the postmodern story by the gospel. As evangelical leaders from previous generations begin to pass the baton to my generation, they have repeatedly emphasized the need simply to preach the gospel. In his autobiography Billy Graham attributes the power of his ministry to this single-minded focus

---

[36]Augustine *Confessions* 10.1.
[37]Taylor, *Sources of the Self*, pp. 139-40.

and commends it to those who would follow in his footsteps. John Stott has similarly emphasized the need to safeguard gospel truths as our highest future priority.[38]

This is certainly wise advice that must be heeded. But it does leave unanswered the question, which rendition of the gospel ought we to preach? The gospel metanarrative is too rich and too alive to be boiled down to a timeless formula that can be repeated verbatim from one generation to the next. The diversity of Scripture itself testifies to the many nuances possible in different situations. Furthermore, the preceding chapters have explored examples of how throughout history different Christians have taken different options in crafting their rendition of the gospel metanarrative. Augustine chose to locate the pivotal point of his narrative in the final judgment, while Aquinas chose the incarnation. Both authors nuanced various aspects of their version to design a custom-made tale to capture their challengers. How do we craft our version of the Story to best captivate the postmodern audience?

While this question ultimately rests within the domain of theologians, the enterprise will be greatly enriched by historical perspective and analysis. Church historians take us out of our own time and thus both open up new possibilities and set helpful boundaries for this creative enterprise. Moreover, comparative analyses of previous responses undoubtedly will yield some general lessons worth heeding. My comparison of Augustine and Aquinas leads me to suggest that any future strategy of capture must take account of three lessons: the newness of our rendition, its relevance and its need for repair.

First, the version of the Story will almost certainly need to be a new one, different from our inherited epochal story. We need to guard against placing an unnecessary value on versions that were designed for past epochs. We have no stake in modernity and its exaltation of rationality,

---

[38]Billy Graham, *Biblical Standards for Evangelists* (Minneapolis: Worldwide, 1984), pp. 36-40. For more of this general perspective, see Billy Graham's autobiography, *Just As I Am* (San Francisco: HarperCollins, 1997); and John Stott, *Guard the Truth* (Downers Grove, Ill.: InterVarsity Press, 1996), pp. 10-13. See also Stott's comments at the fiftieth anniversary celebration of the International Fellowship of Evangelical Students in Memorial Church, Harvard University, October 19, 1997.

objectivity and formulation of truth into universal "laws"—just as Augustine held no stake in the Eternal City and Aquinas held none in the Only City. The key will be to creatively tell stories that are new while still remaining faithful to the gospel in the deepest sense. For all their departures from their inherited epochal stories, Augustine and Aquinas made sure their new tales still fit within the deeper traditions of the church. We are seeking new versions of the Story, not original stories. The latter are usually called heresies.

The need to tell new versions creatively while remaining faithful to the narrative stream of the Story is ultimately an issue not of intellectual brilliance but of spiritual character. Pride is not only the tragic flaw of Rome but also frequently that of the creative. It is no accident that both Augustine and Aquinas were men of deep spirituality and long hours of regular prayer. New storytellers must be open to the creative outpourings of the Spirit while humbly submitting to the authority of the church and Scripture.

Second, we must both shun and seek relevance. The desire to be relevant can be a great trap. Modernity is littered with examples of Christian theologians that so pursued relevance to their epochal challenge that they ended up giving away the biblical Story to the challenger. Teilhard de Chardin so accepted the narrative framework of evolution that his conception of evil departed from the biblical story to fit into evolutionary terms.[39] Similarly, Gustavo Gutiérrez so desired to contextualize the gospel for Latin America in the 1960s that he allowed the secular political theory of "development" to shape even his conception of salvation.[40] We must refuse relevance the way Augustine dismissed Rome to a bit role and the way Aquinas refused to grant Islam apocalyptic status. No epoch is so important that it should begin and end our biblical story. The postmodern epoch simply will not endure as the ultimate framework for our metanarrative. It is quite possible that postmodernism is a doomed

---

[39]See Pierre Teilhard de Chardin, *Activation of Energy* (New York: Harcourt Brace Jovanovich, 1971). For an excellent critique of his conception of evil, see Henri Blocher, *Evil and the Cross* (Downers Grove, Ill.: InterVarsity Press), pp. 22-26.
[40]Gustavo Gutiérrez, *A Theology of Liberation: History, Politics and Salvation* (Maryknoll, N.Y.: Orbis, 1988).

city that will eventually self-deconstruct in a spasm of irrationality. We Christians who have entered it sympathetically will mourn its fate. Like our ancestor Abraham, we will attempt to rescue those residents in "Sodom" who are willing to leave. But we dare not gaze upon it as the Promised Land.

To put it another way, we seek to let the biblical Story ultimately define what is relevant. In my ministry I am constantly looking for ways to tell stories from Scripture that reframe the postmodern story in the biblical metanarrative's terms. For instance, in a weekend conference I engage students in a one-person dramatic presentation of the last days of Jesus' life, drawing out the theme of "collecting" in different characters' lives: Zacchaeus the tax collector, the money changers in the temple, and Judas the betrayer. I weave in narratives of how I as a college student collected different "currencies of self": grades, sex, friends and so on. In the dramatic interweaving of stories I am seeking to present the gospel's narration of "collecting" as the defining story. It is the gospel that best explains my own imploding, conflicting and pathetically tragic stories. And most important, I am presenting Jesus as the only one who can freely offer what "collectors" like myself are seeking.

One may object that pursuing this sort of relevance smacks of the acquiescence to the postmodern context that I just critiqued. After all, the metaphor of sin as "collecting currencies of the self" is not found in that exact formulation in the Bible. But Augustine's depiction of human history as a tale of two cities and Aquinas's characterization of the human soul as on a circular journey are also not explicitly biblical images. This is why the gospel comes to us as story and not as a formula. The material for such depictions has always lain buried in the Story, waiting to be unearthed and fashioned by storytellers like Augustine, Aquinas and those who follow in their footsteps.

In the postmodern epoch some of what we unearth may not fit predictable or pleasant expectations but rather confront us from odd angles. For instance, scholar Phyllis Trible has directed attention to the disturbing biblical "texts of terror," passages of violence and marginalization such as the rape of Tamar. Such passages are usually ignored by modern Christians because they do not fit neatly into any theological formula.

Commenting on Trible's work, J. Richard Middleton and Brian Walsh have argued that such texts warn each generation of readers against turning Scripture into a "totalizing text" that legitimates the status quo, but instead call us to renew our sensitivity to the marginalized of every age.[41]

As the tragic legacies of *City of God* and *Summa contra Gentiles* demonstrate, every text—including the biblical text—is at risk of being flattened into a formula that self-encloses and self-legitimizes passing epochs. But as we foster a correspondence between the postmodern challenge and the biblical narrative, we will recapture neglected corners and angles of Scripture. It may very well be that God's blessing for the church in the postmodern epoch is an adventurous recovery of the unpredictable, three-dimensional nature of his Story. For in those corners and angles we are reminded that this Story defies any epoch's mastery: it is so alive, so encompassing and so true that it can retell the story of every new epoch.

Finally, as we seek to capture the postmodern story, we will need to inspect our narrative nets for places where our version of the Story has broken down. Two places currently most need rhetorical repair: the key act of substitutionary atonement and the final act of the eschaton.

I train my students for evangelism by having them compose and deliver a "three minute gospel story." Generally they sound fluent and engaging while talking about God's redemptive activity from creation to the Fall of humanity and on to the incarnation. However, when they arrive at the point in the story where they are supposed to talk about why Jesus had to die, their story begins to break down. They stumble, trying to present a courtroom story about sin's death penalty, God as judge and Jesus as the punished. This courtroom story clashes with the terms and images they have used in the previous couple of minutes. Sensing the dissonance, they try to pass over this act as quickly as possible.

Watching them, I see what often happens when I am telling the gospel to a nonbeliever: I show how his or her experiences of the self fit into the gospel's understanding of sin. I pique the person's interest with the

---

[41]J. Richard Middleton and Brian J. Walsh, *Truth Is Stranger Than It Used to Be* (Downers Grove, Ill.: InterVarsity Press, 1995), pp. 179-90.

possibility of a wider reality, and then fearing I haven't yet fully said what I am supposed to, I suddenly take out this net called "judicial satisfaction" and fling it hurriedly in his general direction. The net sails right by the nonbeliever, and the person looks at me with some bewilderment.

It is not clear to me how our current strategy of presenting of the cross actually captures the postmodern story. Scripture contains several metaphors for the atonement, such as the sacrificial, the military, the judicial and the familial. Church history reveals that the atonement has been presented differently in different epochs. In the early church the doctrine was told as a completion of the Jewish practice of sacrifice: hence "the blood of the Lamb" that washes humanity clean. In the medieval epoch the sacrifice of Jesus was retold as a ransom for our captivity, which fit with feudal experiences of serfdom, as well as the practice of buying freedom for soldiers seized in combat. In the modern epoch the story of the cross as judicial satisfaction for the divine principles of justice spoke to modernity's conception of universal and principled truths. Within much of the church today, the metaphors and illustrative stories of this narrative framework still dominate presentations of the cross. There is, of course, profound truth in the judicial narrative—it is, after all, found in several passages of Scripture—and it should not be discarded. But to capture the postmodern's attention, satisfy his or her deepest desire and resolve his or her tragic flaw, we must also creatively work in the other biblical metaphors to present the atonement for our epoch. [42]

Depicting the atonement in creative and biblically faithful ways is especially crucial because the cross plants itself at the heart of the tragic tension of the postmodern story. The postmodern challenge truthfully reveals the human condition: the radical doubt that afflicts our understanding and the suffering inflicted on the marginalized. Awareness of this condition so occupies the postmodern story that it relentlessly strips away cover stories that seek to hide or minimize the harsh reality. Yet for

---

[42]For classic theological and historical analysis of the judicial version of the atonement, see Gustaf Aulén, *Christus Victor*, trans. A. G. Herbert (London: SPCK, 1953). See also Colin Gunton, *The Actuality: A Study of Metaphor, Rationality and the Christian Tradition* (Grand Rapids, Mich.: Eerdmans, 1989).

all its sensitivity to the doubt of the knower and the cries of the marginal, it can offer no real balm. The postmodern story is stuck here.

The cross stands as God's unexpected yet satisfying resolution of this tension. In Christ, God too refuses to minimize human doubt or suffering. In fact, he purposefully endures the full brunt of this human condition. At the cross, God himself undergoes the severest crisis of doubt: "My God, my God, why hast thou forsaken me?" (Mt 27:46 KJV). At the cross, God himself is crucified as the absolutely marginalized One. But the forces of doubt and marginalization cannot separate the Son from the Father. At the very climax of the cross, their mutual knowledge and love overcome all. As a result, all of humanity is gathered into that familial embrace.

This welcome into the family of Father, Son and Holy Spirit completes the postmodern epoch's unresolved story. This family is where doubters are reassured and the marginalized are welcomed. It is the experience of God's love. Postmoderns—as the first generation to experience the widespread breakdown of the family—long for this experience. Their personal stories often are filled with the doubt and pain caused by divorce, abuse and other family dysfunction. The postmodern yearning for true family must be addressed by our epoch's rendition of the gospel.

Space does not permit me to do anything here other than suggest the broad contours of such a postmodern proclamation. The enterprise is a delicate one, as it requires emphasizing aspects of the gospel metanarrative that may have been neglected by a previous epoch while at the same time not losing important truths safeguarded by the emphasis of earlier times. For instance, how does an evangelist tell the familial narrative of the atonement and yet still include the necessary qualifications found in the judicial narrative? And how does the final product still cohere in the way a story must cohere: with a plot, a central dramatic action, a consistent metaphorical universe and other basic narrative elements? Clearly, this enterprise will require the joint efforts of Christian theologians, evangelists, preachers and artists.

Recovering the conclusion of our gospel story will also be critical. Reading *City of God* and *Summa contra Gentiles*, one is struck by the importance of eschatology in both their metanarratives. The vividness of Augustine's and Aquinas's descriptions of the consummation of history stand in sharp contrast to the neglect of this subject in the church today. With the exception of certain fundamentalist fringes, the average contemporary church rarely hears sermons on the final judgment or any other aspect of Christian eschatology.

Our eschatological poverty is another aspect of our inheritance from modernity. As the late social historian Christopher Lasch pointed out, most mainline Protestant denominations in the last two centuries essentially embraced modernity's confidence in progress via the right social programs and politics. As a result, the doctrine of Christ's return fell by the wayside as liberals came to believe they themselves could perfect society to its ultimate end.[43]

The fundamentalist wing of the church rightly rejected this vision of history. But in trying to hold on to Christ's return, it ended up unconsciously embracing modernity in another way: in the modern preoccupation with scientific precision and forecasting. Thus fundamentalist theologians like the dispensationalists and their popularizers like Hal Lindsey charted elaborate and often competing timetables for the end times.[44]

Evangelicals embraced modernity in a third way. Modernity assigned religion to a purely private realm, and evangelicalism has tended to accept this private space quite willingly. Therefore, to the extent evangelicalism serves up any conception of the end, it tends to be fairly bareboned, restricted to questions of individual salvation. Without a robust vision of the wider world's future, it is not surprising that evangelicals tend to concentrate on personal belief in the present.

All three of these visions deviate significantly from the biblical narratives of the eschaton. For example, in the parables of the master returning to the servants (Lk 12:35-48), Jesus depicts an end ushered in by God and not by human striving, on a timetable no one can scientifically pre-

---

[43]Christopher Lasch, *The True and Only Heaven* (New York: W. W. Norton, 1991), pp. 369-77.
[44]Interestingly, Augustine steadfastly refused to give in to the desire for preciseness in his telling of the eschaton. For instance, see *COG* 10.19, p. 934; *COG* 21.9, p. 985.

dict and covering a range of relationships in society.

Not surprisingly, the liberal, fundamentalist and evangelical visions of the end have reached something of a dead end in the postmodern epoch. The disasters of the two world wars decimated the liberal vision of progress, while the fundamentalist movement eventually imploded in its self-enclosed conflict over rival timetables. The evangelical vision, while appealing to Western individualism, also falls prey to individualism's inability to draw the self out of its narrow world into a broader reality. As a result, the contemporary church no longer ventures a word about the consummation of history.

But a satisfying conclusion is crucial to a compelling tale. And a clear conception of the end strongly influences how one tells the entire story. This basic need for a robust conclusion points to yet another unresolved tension in the postmodern story. As a worldview postmodernism seeks to deconstruct all previous overarching goals to history, but itself lacks the resources to provide an alternative ending. As a historical moment the epoch seems to embody this paralysis. Political visions of the end, like the socialist utopia, have been demolished, and the postwar faith in unlimited economic growth wobbles. The usual voices have fallen mute, but no one else possesses the confidence to speak up. We slouch, disillusioned and cynical about all the failed dreams littering our landscape, and lower our sights to simply getting by with what lies before us. Our epoch seems to be exhausted of hope.

A key contest of our epoch will be waged between those who can summon the nerve to tell a hopeful conclusion. Computer and communications technology—almost alone of all secular fields—still exhibits the energy to propose some bright vision of the future. Of course these visions are mostly recycled heresies. For instance, technology increasingly advocates an end akin either to the ancient Gnostic vision, where we will escape our bodies into some virtual reality, or to the ancient pantheist vision, where we will be completely absorbed into each other in some internetworked sea of information. Nevertheless, despite their basic unoriginality, technology mavens' willingness even to talk about the future is an important source of their growing influence in our broader culture.

The preachers, evangelists and scholars of the church certainly must participate in the epochal storytelling contest. This means recapturing all the angular dimensions of our conclusion, such as the final judgment. Christian culture tends to sidestep this seemingly harsh part of our story; we would be jarred to walk through a Christian bookstore and see next to the ubiquitous pastel poster of "Footprints" another poster depicting "The Sheep and the Goats." We are secretly embarrassed by this doctrine's judgmental quality—a quality tantamount to the unforgivable sin in postmodern culture.

But Augustine and Aquinas both point to the final judgment as the final revelation of the resolution already achieved in Christ. Augustine looks forward eagerly to that day when the violent pride of humankind will finally be swallowed up, Aquinas to that moment when human beings finally discern God truly and fully. We storytellers must similarly lift the postmodern's eyes beyond the current horizon to this future. It is true that the powerful still oppress the weak before our very eyes, and it is true that our epistemology still resembles seeing though a glass darkly. This is why we invite all to live in anticipation of the judgment that will bring justice and clarity. If postmodern persons are to recover true hope, they must recover the expectation of the final judgment.

Historically, the telling of the final judgment has transformed entire epochs. We can draw inspiration from an illustrious line of ancestors besides Augustine and Aquinas. The early church so boldly preached the expectation of the Lord's imminent return that this tiny, persecuted minority reshaped a worldwide pagan empire into a Christian one. In the medieval era a young poet opposed a corrupt church and endured banishment, loss of possessions and threat of death. In exile Dante created the *Divine Comedy*, a work that depicted the end so vividly that his vision shaped that age's artistic and literary worlds. In nineteenth-century America abolitionists like William Lloyd Garrison preached the judgment of God with such fire that President Lincoln admitted he shuddered at what God would do if slavery continued, and Union troops marched to battle singing a hymn about the grapes of God's wrath. And in the twentieth century, Oxford don C. S. Lewis faced a scientific modernity that had grown, in Max Weber's terms, "disenchanted with the universe." Lewis responded with, of all things, a series of children's books that has reenchanted millions, leading them to the final chapter when the Lion returns to fight the "Last Battle."

## Our Future Storytellers

If lessons like these need to inform our future stories, the final question must be, who will tell them? The life stories of Augustine and Aquinas suggest that our best future storytellers will have "bilingual" training. As the church considers how it trains its theologians and historians, pastors and teachers, it needs to consider how to expose them to the language and terms of the postmodern epoch.

Augustine's and Aquinas's life stories also warn the church today to pay attention to its margins. Creative insight will often come from the fringes of the epoch, where independent perspective is possible. Where then are our equivalents of North Africa and the mendicant movements? The Western church especially must pay attention to and cultivate voices from the Third World. In places like India the church has been dealing with issues such as religious pluralism for far longer than we have in the West. Thinkers there have already shown how from the fringes they can offer unique perspectives on Western culture itself.[45] In this regard one danger of our postmodern epoch is the globalization of culture via new technology. The Internet, Hollywood and worldwide commercialism are all fast eradicating the distinctiveness of the periphery with a bland, mostly Western culture. The church must guard against allowing such technologies to obliterate the future stories of future storytellers.

The margins of the church will also most likely produce storytellers who have lived the postmodern story "from the inside." Like Augustine, those who convert to Christianity relatively late in life will still retain the language of the nonbelieving culture. In particular, our most compelling storytellers will be those who have suffered firsthand the tragic flaws of the postmodern story and thus posses the empathy and insight necessary to "take every thought captive."

---

[45]Lesslie Newbigin's works stand as prime examples of this sort of critique from the margins. For other examples see Vinoth Ramachandra, *Gods That Fail: Modern Idolatry and Christian Mission* (Downers Grove, Ill.: InterVarsity Press, 1997); and *Recovery of Mission: Beyond the Pluralist Paradigm* (Grand Rapids, Mich.: Eerdmans, 1997).

Every year, Christian foundations invest large sums of money to cultivate the voices of Christianity that will have broad future influence. In the hope of finding the next Augustine, Aquinas or C. S. Lewis, grants are given to Christians studying at the most elite universities and seminaries. The reality is that the majority of the recipients are Western white males bearing the impeccable credentials of a Christian background. But if I were to imagine what the Augustine, Aquinas or Lewis of the postmodern epoch might look like, I might picture a single woman who immigrated to the West from Pakistan, had an abortion before becoming a follower of Jesus and is now a budding filmmaker.

In the end, though, our most convincing stories will emerge from the everyday lives of everyday Christians. In his letter to the Corinthians, the apostle Paul reminds everyone that the most important correspondences are the ones "written on our hearts, to be known and read by all . . . written not with ink but with the Spirit of the living God, not on tablets of stone but on tablets of human hearts" (2 Cor 3:2-3). Nothing is more captivating to a nonbeliever in any epoch than hearing a story from a friend which reveals how Jesus has entered, retold and captured the storyteller's life. Our best words to epochal challengers ultimately come not in some creative philosophical structure or brilliant historical analysis. Our best words are spoken in the language of testimony. It is no accident that Augustine's *Confessions* is far more widely read than is *City of God*. And, as mentioned, Aquinas is remembered as *Saint* Thomas because of testimony to his transformed life. As Aquinas noted, "The divine truth—exceeding the human intellect—descends on us in the manner of revelation, not, however, as something made clear to be seen, but as something spoken in words to be believed."[46] We testify to a grand Story, a love story of suffering and hope, of judgment and redemption. The beautiful Word of that Story is ours, and we invite all to hear and believe.

---

[46]*SCG* 4.1.5, p. 37.

# Appendix

## *Summa contra Gentiles* & Missions

$M$Y READING OF *SUMMA CONTRA GENTILES* as Aquinas's response to the epochal challenge of Islam runs counter to the latest trend in academic scholarship on *SCG*. A number of influential scholars have recently rejected the long-held belief that Aquinas composed *SCG* with a missiological intent. This appendix represents my engagement with this position. Fellow students and scholars of Aquinas are my primary audience here, and general readers who already accept my account of Aquinas's intentions in *SCG* can feel free to skip this somewhat "in-house" discussion. However, this discussion may be illuminating for anyone interested more generally in the relationship between Christian scholarship and missions.

The most famous Aquinas scholar to reject the missiological intent of *SCG* is philosopher Norman Kretzmann. His 1997 book *The Metaphysics of Theism: Aquinas's Natural Theology in* Summa contra Gentiles *I* rests on this rejection, and he begins the book with a lengthy justification for his view.[1]

While he cites a number of other and older works on the issue, Kretzmann stands as the most influential voice by virtue of his preeminence in

---

[1]Norman Kretzmann, *The Metaphysics of Theism* (New York: Clarendon, 1997), pp. 43-53.

the philosophical community: for instance, he served as coeditor of *The Cambridge Companion to Aquinas*, and it was he who was asked to compose the entry on Aquinas in the prestigious *Routledge Encyclopedia of Philosophy*. Thus for convenience' sake I will use the term the "Kretzmann school" to denote the scholars seeking to detach *SCG* from the epochal challenge of Islam. While these scholars have different perspectives on Aquinas with regards to other questions, their arguments on this specific issue are similar. I take as the representative voices of the school Kretzmann himself, Mark D. Jordan and Thomas Hibbs.[2]

To review, I hold the classic view of *SCG*'s historical occasion: that it was written by Aquinas in response to a request from Ramon of Penyaforte, a missionary to Islam. This view has been widely accepted for centuries and has only come under attack in the past few decades. The classic view has dominated for so long for the simple reason that the best and most contemporary historical account of *SCG*'s origins presents it. This account, which I introduced in chapter one, is by the Dominican chronicler Peter Marsilius. Marsilius recorded the memories of Ramon of Penyaforte about James I of Aragon—not, interestingly enough, about Aquinas himself. Hence there is no sign of a hagiographic inflation of Aquinas; the account has the flavor of a historical aside. It is told within another specific memory of Ramon that is dated specifically to Christmas 1274, probably less than twenty years after Ramon actually made the request to Aquinas.[3]

A great deal of historical specificity also surrounds Marsilius's text itself. It evidently was finished on April 2, 1313, about forty years after Aquinas's death and probably fifty-four to fifty-six years after he began *SCG*. Despite centuries of Thomist historical scholarship, no one has found a more contemporary or reliable account of *SCG*'s origins. In fact, no one has ever found *any* alternative account attested by any historical

---

[2]I should note that René A. Gauthier, in his *Thomas d'Aquin: "Contra Gentiles," Livre Premier* (Lyons, France: P. Lethielleux, 1961), was probably one of the earliest leading voices of this line of thought. However, the scholars I listed are much more recent and encapsulate Gauthier's work on this matter.

[3]Mark D. Jordan, "The Protreptic Structure of the *Summa contra Gentiles*," in *The Thomist* 50 (1986): 175. For the dating of *SCG* I'm relying on John Finnis, *Aquinas* (Oxford: Oxford University Press, 1998), p. xix.

document. By most historical and textual standards, Marsilius's text seems quite reliable. Even Jordan, a member of the Kretzmann school, must admit: "There have been some textual questions about this passage [by Marsilius], but none is unanswerable. Let the text stand as received."[4]

So why has there been a recent spate of attacks on the classic view? Below I suggest some possible underlying reasons. But the most important task here is to address the substance of the debate. Notably, the overwhelming bulk of arguments advanced by the Kretzmann school relies not on historical evidence but on exegetical assumptions. More specifically, their arguments comprise two main components: (a) their perceived reading of the genre and structure of *SCG* and (b) their assumptions of what the genre and structure should have been if the *SCG* truly was written in response to the epochal challenge of Islam.

The most often repeated claim is that if Aquinas was writing with Islam in mind, he should have included citations of Muslim texts. Hibbs makes a great deal of the fact that the standard Dominican missiological strategy required "careful analysis of [the adversary's] position" by recourse to the adversary's religious texts.[5] Jordan cites how Ramon himself set up a debate against Jews in 1263 (note that this is *before* he would have received the completed *SCG*) by using Jewish texts.[6] Hibbs and Jordan argue that since Aquinas doesn't cite Muslim texts in similar fashion, Aquinas is not following standard Dominican missiological strategy. Therefore, they conclude, *SCG* is not a missiological text.[7]

The weakness of this argument should be apparent to the reader of the preceding chapters. First, Aquinas does cite Averroës and Avicenna profusely—and both of these are Islamic authorities, Averroës even being a *qadi*, a religious judge—a fact that Kretzmann essentially ignores, only vaguely alluding to it in a footnote.[8] True, Aquinas doesn't cite the Qur'an itself, but that is because he has declared in book 1 that his strategy is to

---

[4]Jordan, "Protreptic Structure," p. 175.

[5]Thomas Hibbs, *Dialectic and Narrative in Aquinas: An Interpretation of the "Summa contra Gentiles"* (Notre Dame, Ind.: University of Notre Dame Press, 1995), p. 182.

[6]Jordan, "Protreptic Structure," p. 177.

[7]Hibbs, *Dialectic and Narrative*, p. 182.

[8]Kretzmann, *Metaphysics of Theism*, p. 50 n

meet his adversaries on the common ground of reason—especially via Aristotle—and not on the "incommensurate" ground of conflicting religious texts.

Second, assuming Ramon really did make his plea to Aquinas for help, wouldn't it be reasonable to surmise that Ramon felt he needed something different, that he recognized that the standard Dominican missiological strategy was ineffective? To show, as Jordan does, that Ramon's missiological strategy before receiving *SCG* differed from *SCG*'s strategy hardly disproves Marsilius's account; on the contrary, it suggests that Ramon was right in hoping that Aquinas could offer something new. And why should it be surprising that Aquinas—an obviously creative thinker—would respond with a strategy that differed from the standard strategies of the day? The Kretzmann school's reasoning that Aquinas should have followed the standard strategy if he had any missiological intent simply makes no sense.

Third, when Jordan highlights the difference between Ramon's strategy with the Jews and Aquinas's strategy in *SCG*, he is actually confirming the distinctive focus on Islam that animates *SCG*. In the opening to *SCG*, Aquinas himself explains why he wouldn't follow Ramon's strategy with the Jews in responding to Islam:

> The Mohammedans and the pagans do not agree with us in accepting the authority of any Scripture, by which they may be convinced of their error. Thus, against the Jews we are able to argue by means of the Old Testament, while against heretics we are able to argue by means of the New Testament. But the Mohammedans and the pagans accept neither the one nor the other.

"We must, therefore," Aquinas concludes, "have recourse to the natural reason, to which all men are forced to give their assent."[9] Aquinas himself explains quite clearly why the epochal challenge of Islam required a different strategy.

As far as I can tell, almost all of the Kretzmann school's arguments are variations of this basic form: If Aquinas really had a missiological intent, then *SCG* would have been written like A; since it is written like B, it

---

[9]*SCG* 1.2.3, p. 62.

must not be missiological. This sort of counterfactual reasoning is notoriously open to abuse. For instance, Kretzmann defines apologetics as "answering objections to the faith," which is a "reactive enterprise." Since Aquinas is "initiating" in *SCG*, Kretzmann argues he could not possibly be doing apologetics, and therefore *SCG* is not a missiological text.[10] Kretzmann thus subjects Aquinas to a very narrow definition of apologetics and makes a sweeping equation between that definition and missiological intent.

Kretzmann makes numerous similar leaps of reasoning that are tenuous at best, incomprehensible at worst. For example, one line of argument runs as follows: (1) all theological textbooks written by Aquinas should begin by discussing God's nature, because that is how he structures his later *Summa Theologica*; (2) *SCG* does not adhere to this structure, for it postpones all trinitarian discussions to book 4; (3) *SCG* is thus not a theological textbook—which then leads to the conclusion that (4) *SCG* could not possibly be aimed at instructing missionaries.[11] Kretzmann's procrustean definitions (e.g., all of Aquinas's theological textbooks must take a specific structure) and reasoning (e.g., non-"textbook" automatically means nonmissiological) lop off the possibilities that Aquinas could choose different literary structures for different occasions and that he could have pursued missiological intents without writing in the textbook genre. And as to the specific issue of why Aquinas postpones introducing the Trinity, I believe I present a more compelling explanation rooted in his strategy of engaging Islam's primary doctrinal objection to the gospel (see pp. 129-30).

Another rather bizarre argument runs as follows: (1) *SCG* presents a flurry of arguments; (2) Aquinas states in *Summa Theologica* (again, written several years after *SCG*) that a book with too many arguments is an unsuitable genre for beginners; (3) therefore *SCG* could not be a textbook for beginner missionaries—which leads to the conclusion that (4) *SCG* could not have had a missiological intent.[12] For the sake of space, I will ignore the several logical fallacies perpetrated here, but suffice it to

---

[10]Kretzmann, *Metaphysics of Theism*, p. 47.
[11]Ibid., pp. 45-46.
[12]Ibid., p. 46.

say that premise 3 certainly does not lead to conclusion 4. Kretzmann ignores the possibility that Aquinas, like Augustine, may have taken a specific request from a missionary (one who, by the way, was decidedly not a "beginner") to address broader and more complex missiological concerns.

Kretzmann clearly is aware of this possibility, since he frequently cites his colleague Anthony Kenny, a noted Thomist.[13] Kenny accepts *SCG*'s missiological intent, although he argues that its focus was not just Muslims but any "people who are not Christians, who may be Muslims or Jews or atheists."[14] While Kenny's view is compatible with mine, I would still argue that Aquinas had a particular emphasis on Muslims in *SCG*. "Atheists" as a defined grouping was nonexistent in his day; and as noted above, in missions to Jews Aquinas advises a very different rhetorical strategy (relying on the Old Testament) than the one he advances in *SCG*. Nevertheless, my main point is that Kretzmann seems especially insistent on rejecting any missiological intent, even ignoring a colleague's more diffuse missiological reading. Such an insistent interpretation unfortunately leads Kretzmann to pursue contorted lines of reasoning.

The twists of logic Kretzmann employs are matched by the exegetical violence he inflicts on the text itself. Having staked his historical claim about *SCG*'s original intention on exegetical grounds, he cannot faithfully protect that ground. His rejection of the missiological context of *SCG* does not lead to a more coherent reading of the text; on the contrary, he must drastically sever its unity to maintain his claim.

Here we get into his underlying agenda. From the first page, he states his belief that "a great deal—not all—of theology's traditional subject-matter is really continuous with philosophy's subject matter, and ought to be integrated with it in practice."[15] Thus Kretzmann is eager to appropriate Aquinas as a philosopher as opposed to a theologian-missiologist, or at least to shift Aquinas further toward the philosophy camp. His opening chapter makes clear that this agenda depends on portraying *SCG* as an exercise in natural theology. "I'm convinced that natural theology," he states, "still offers the best route by which philosophers can, as philoso-

---

[13]Ibid., p. 273.
[14]Anthony Kenny, *Aquinas on Mind* (London: Routledge, 1993), p. 13.
[15]Kretzmann, *Metaphysics of Theism*, p. 1.

phers, approach theological propositions."[16] Indeed, this agenda of positioning Aquinas away from the theology camp is present in the older works that Kretzmann cites to support his view.[17]

Given this agenda, it is not surprising that Kretzmann seeks to expunge any explicitly theological intentions like missions to Islam. But this leads him to one terribly shaky exegetical move after another. For instance, he claims that books 1-3 "contain nothing contrary to Islam." Therefore we must rule out any missiological intention: "If Aquinas had intended SCG as a manual for missionaries to educated Muslims, Jews, or Christian heretics, he would have wasted the enormous effort represented in the 366 chapters of Books I-III. For the practical purposes of proselytizing he should have undertaken no more than the contents of Book IV."[18]

This sort of counterfactual reasoning is fatally flawed, especially in its reading of the text and its derived conclusions. First of all, Kretzmann makes that sweeping claim about the first three books "containing nothing contrary to Islam" but attaches a footnote: "My views on Islamic doctrine are pretty ill-informed, and I would welcome correction on this point."[19] I believe chapter four of this book offers such a correction. But it is perplexing that Kretzmann could build his whole book on a rejection of the relationship of SCG to Islam while being admittedly ill-informed on Islam.[20]

Even more important, to reason that if Aquinas had proselytizing in mind he "should have undertaken no more than the contents of Book IV" is to completely miss Aquinas's rhetorical strategy. Such an argument insists that Aquinas should have been just like the standard polemicists of the day: standing on a Muslim street corner and condemning his audi-

---

[16]Ibid., pp. 21-22.

[17]Ibid., p. 44. See, for example, M. D. Chenu, *Introduction à l'étude de saint Thomas d'Aquin* (Paris: J. Vrin, 1950), pp. 247-51.

[18]Kretzmann, *Metaphysics of Theism*, p. 50.

[19]Ibid.

[20]Granting Kretzmann as much leeway as possible, I can only assume that he is relying on sharply distinguishing between Islam and the Islamic philosophical writings that Aquinas laboriously critiques throughout SCG 1-3. Separating the two so totally is a very shaky move given the historical realities of the epoch I have outlined in chapter two.

ence's beliefs by spewing biblical passages. To claim that accepting a missiological intent means Aquinas wasted the effort in books 1-3 is to blindly ignore the possibility that these books were written specifically so book 4's theology could serve as a dramatic climax awaited by the audience. But Kretzmann relegates to a footnote the possibility that all four books of *SCG* are organically united, calling it merely "an interesting alternative."[21]

Since that alternative remains hidden in a footnote and unexplored by Kretzmann, he must forge ahead exegetically with his agenda. What then, is his proposed relationship between books 1-3 and book 4? He can offer no answer. Book 4's explicitly theological content—which as I argue is missiological as well—sticks out glaringly from the natural theology framework. Recognizing this discomfiting reality, Kretzmann says that his exegesis is "meant to apply only to what [Aquinas] does in the first three books."[22] Thus he lops off the entire climactic book 4 of *SCG!* It is no accident that his book's subtitle is *Aquinas's Natural Theology in "Summa contra Gentiles" I,* leaving even books 2-3 dangling. Yet what is most needed by the exegetical community on *SCG* is some sort of unifying reading (see chapter one). Kretzmann's exegetical move is comparable to a modern Shakespearean scholar who while claiming to know the Bard's intentions in *Hamlet* issues a demurral: "Of course, my reading only applies to act 1, maybe 2 and 3, and for my purposes let us ignore act 4 and its climax altogether."

The redeeming element of the Kretzmann school argument, in my opinion, is the historical claim that the approach of *SCG* was never significantly adopted by Dominican missionaries. This is true, as noted above in chapter five. But Aquinas's failure to spread his unique missiological strategy does not necessarily lead to the conclusion that the Kretzmann school draws: that he never intended to have a missiological impact in the first place.[23] The hopes of many great thinkers did not translate into success, and I have tried to explain why this was the case with *SCG* (see pp. 140-41).

---

[21]Kretzmann, *Metaphysics of Theism,* p. 50.
[22]Ibid., p. 48.
[23]See Hibbs, *Dialectic and Narrative,* pp. 179-80.

That missionaries failed to carry on *SCG*'s accomplishments also leads Hibbs and others to question the veracity of Peter Marsilius's account of Ramon of Penyaforte's request to Aquinas. Seizing on Marsilius's description of *SCG* as "held to be without equal in its field," Hibbs argues that this phrase represents "the gravest objection" to the reliability of Marsilius's account.[24] The argument seems to be that if *SCG* was truly without equal in the missions field, it should have been replicated more. Again, this is weak reasoning. *SCG* may be without equal precisely because it was so distinctive and brilliant—and thus difficult to replicate. Again, to return to my earlier analogy, Hibbs's objection is like a modern Shakespearean scholar objecting to the veracity of a seventeenth-century account praising William Shakespeare as without equal, simply because that period produced so few other authors writing plays as brilliant as *Hamlet*.

Moreover, Jordan himself documents how one leading missionary to Islam, Raymond Marti, did change his strategy after receiving the *SCG*. Whereas Marti had totally ignored Aristotle previous to receiving Aquinas's work, afterward his writings show direct borrowing from *SCG*. Jordan dismisses this example because "Marti uses Thomas chiefly to combat errors arising from the reading of Aristotle and his followers. . . . When it comes to a detailed consideration of the claims and counterclaims of sacred writings . . . borrowings from Thomas almost disappear." But according to my reading of *SCG*, that is exactly as should be predicted, since Aquinas's missiological strategy was to "enter" and "retell" Islam via Aristotle and avoid incommensurate argumentation between "claims and counter-claims of sacred writings."

Like others, Jordan unfortunately assumes that philosophical discussion of Aristotle automatically excludes missiological intent. Thus Jordan concludes "it was precisely the *non-missionary* parts of [Marti] which benefited most from a reading of the *Contra Gentiles*."[25] Once again, the critic misses precisely what was the intention and unique contribution of *SCG*: that Aquinas sought to use Aristotle as common ground for missio-

---

[24]Ibid., p. 180.
[25]Jordan, "Protreptic Structure," p. 179, emphasis mine.

logical engagement. It seems at least one practicing missionary of the day caught that vision, even if Jordan and other modern scholars refuse to accept it.

This scholarly unbelief seems untenable even if we set aside evidence like Marsilius's account or exegesis of *SCG* itself. Even if we accept a certain agnosticism about Aquinas's exact circumstances and intentions in writing *SCG*, it still seems inconceivable that the epochal challenge of Islam did not serve as the most significant background to his work. Some general facts undisputed by any: the Crusades are raging at this time as a defining political issue; the rediscovery of Aristotle by the West comes via Islam; the effect of Aristotle on Western Christendom's philosophical self-confidence is epochal; whereas before *SCG* Aquinas had confined himself to commenting on explicitly Christian literature, after writing *SCG* he suddenly expends enormous energy on responding to Aristotle.[26] Some more personal facts about Aquinas that are also undisputed: his Dominican order is passionately committed to missions to Islam; Aquinas is in relationship with such missionaries; Aquinas himself must have had significant contact with Muslims in Naples; and mention of "the Mohammedans" does recur in *SCG*, especially in the first chapters where he is outlining his intentions for the work. Finally, the year he finishes *SCG* he writes a short tract, *De rationibus fidei contra Saracenos, Graecomes et Armenos*, which is (as even Jordan agrees) written with the Saracen challenge in mind.[27] Thus a heavy burden of proof must be borne by anyone claiming that Aquinas was not seriously thinking about the Islamic challenge while writing the *SCG*.

Why has the scholarly community been so intent on rejecting Aquinas's missiological intent? I would not hazard to guess what lies in the heart of any individual scholar. But I will conclude by risking some generalizations. For some time now the secular environment has turned increasingly hostile to the notion of evangelism and missions. In our postmodern and relativistic times, the secular academic community has been particularly vociferous in denouncing Christian attempts to "proselytize"

---

[26] See Kretzmann's own chronology in *Metaphysics of Theism*, pp. 255-62.
[27] John Finnis, *Aquinas* (Oxford: Oxford University Press, 1998), p. xix; Jordan, "Protreptic Structure," pp. 180-81.

other religious communities. Faced with such a hostile climate, we Christian scholars have tended to shy away from supporting, much less participating in, the church's missionary enterprise. Detached from missions ourselves, we produce scholarship that follows suit. When examining Aquinas from such a removed position, we find discomfiting the vision of this scholar so passionately engaged in controversial (even in his day) missionary work. He does not serve our preferences for academic discourse around more acceptable issues.

The scholarly picture of Aquinas that emerges from the recent literature seems but a self-depiction: safely making abstract inquiries in academic conferences far removed from the costlier work of modern-day Ramons of Penyaforte. There is some value to scholarly detachment and inquiry which I do not want to disparage. But if we want to truly follow this great thinker and his thoughts, we should be clear on what the real questions are. The true question for scholars is not whether Thomas Aquinas was committed to the missionary proclamation of the gospel. The answer to that seems clear. The real question is whether we will be.

# Select Bibliography

**Augustine**

Augustine. *City of God.* Translated by Henry Bettenson, introduction by John O'Meara. London: Penguin, 1987.

———. *Confessions.* Translated by R. S. Pine-Coffin. New York: Penguin, 1987.

———. *De doctrina christiana.* Edited by D. W. Robertson. New York: Bobbs Merrill, 1958.

Brown, Peter. *Augustine of Hippo.* Berkeley: University of California Press, 1969.

———. *Religion and Society in the Age of St. Augustine.* New York: Harper & Row, 1972.

———. *Society and the Holy in Late Antiquity.* Berkeley: University of California Press, 1982.

———. *The World of Late Antiquity.* London: Thames and Hudson, 1971.

Fortin, Ernest. *Classical Christianity and the Political Order.* Lanham, Md.: Rowman & Littlefield, 1996.

MacMullen, Ramsay. *Christianity and Paganism in the Fourth to Eighth Centuries.* New Haven, Conn.: Yale University Press, 1997.

———. *Christianizing the Roman Empire.* New Haven, Conn.: Yale University Press, 1984.

Markus, Robert. *Christianity in the Roman World.* London: Thames and Hudson, 1974.

———. *The End of Ancient Christianity.* Cambridge: Cambridge University Press, 1990.

———. *Saeculum.* London: Cambridge University Press, 1970.

O'Donnell, James J. *Augustine.* Boston: Twayne, 1985.


**Aquinas**

Aertsen, Jan. *Nature and Creature: St. Thomas Aquinas's Way of Thought.* Translated by H. D. Morton. Leiden: E. J. Brill, 1988.

Aquinas, Thomas. *Summa contra Gentiles.* Books 1-4, Translated, with introduction and notes, by Anton C. Pegis et al. Notre Dame, Ind.: University of Notre Dame Press, 1975.

Aristotle. *Poetics.* In *The Works of Aristotle.* Translated by W. D. Ross. London: Oxford University Press, 1949.

Cahill, Thomas. *How the Irish Saved Civilization.* New York: Doubleday, 1995.

Chesterton, G. K. *Saint Thomas Aquinas: The Dumb Ox.* New York: Doubleday, 1956.

Constable, Giles. *The Reformation of the 12th Century.* Cambridge: Cambridge University Press, 1996.

Daniel, Norman. *Islam and the West.* Edinburgh: Edinburgh University Press, 1960.

Fletcher, Richard. *The Barbarian Conversion.* New York: Henry Holt, 1997.

Gilson, Étienne. *The Spirit of Mediaeval Philosophy.* Notre Dame, Ind.: University of Notre Dame Press, 1991.

Finnis, John. *Aquinas.* Oxford: Oxford University Press, 1998.

Hibbs, Thomas. *Dialectic and Narrative in Aquinas: An Interpretation of the "Summa contra Gentiles."* Notre Dame, Ind.: University of Notre Dame Press, 1995.

Kedar, Benjamin Z. *Crusade and Mission*. Princeton, N.J.: Princeton University Press, 1984.

Kenny, Anthony. *Aquinas on Mind*. London: Routledge, 1993.

Kretzmann, Norman. *The Metaphysics of Theism: Aquinas's Natural Theology in Summa contra Gentiles I*. New York: Clarendon, 1997.

Kretzmann, Norman, and Eleonore Stump. *The Cambridge Companion to Aquinas*. Cambridge: Cambridge University Press, 1993.

MacIntyre, Alasdair. *Three Rival Versions of Moral Enquiry*. Notre Dame, Ind.: University of Notre Dame Press, 1990.

——. *Whose Justice? Which Rationality?* Notre Dame, Ind.: University of Notre Dame Press, 1988.

McInerny, Ralph. *A First Glance at St. Thomas Aquinas*. Notre Dame, Ind.: University of Notre Dame Press, 1990.

——. *St. Thomas Aquinas*. Boston: Twayne, 1977.

Naipaul, V. S. *Beyond Belief: Islamic Excursions Among the Converted People*. New York: Random House, 1998.

Watt, William M. *Muslim-Christian Encounters*. London: Routledge, 1991

## Postmodernity and General Works

Armour, Ellen. *Deconstruction, Feminist Theology and the Problem of Difference*. Chicago: University of Chicago Press, 1999.

Behe, Michael. *Darwin's Black Box: The Biochemical Challenge to Evolution*. New York: Simon & Schuster, 1998.

Bellah, Robert, et al. *Habits of the Heart: Individualism and Commitment in American Life*. Berkeley: University of California Press, 1996 (original ed. 1985).

Berger, Peter. *The Sacred Canopy: Elements of a Sociological Theory of Religion*. Garden City, N.Y.: Doubleday, 1967.

Berger, Peter, and Thomas Luckmann. *The Social Construction of Reality*. Garden City, N.Y.: Doubleday, 1966.

Buckley, Michael J. *At the Origins of Modern Atheism*. New Haven, Conn.: Yale University Press, 1987.

Capps, Donald. *The Depleted Self*. Minneapolis: Fortress, 1993.

Derrida, Jacques. *Of Grammatology*. Baltimore: Johns Hopkins University Press, 1977.

——. *Speech and Phenomena*. Translated by David Allison. Evanston, Ill.: Northwestern University Press, 1972.

Ellul, Jacques. *Humiliation of the Word*. Translated by J. M. Hanks. Grand Rapids, Mich.: Eerdmans, 1985.

Foucault, Michel. *Discipline and Punish*. New York: Vintage, 1979.

Gramsci, Antonio. *Selections from the Prison Notebooks*. New York: International Publishers, 1989.

Hauerwas, Stanley. *A Community of Character*. Notre Dame, Ind.: University of Notre Dame Press, 1981.

Hunter, James Davison. *Before the Shooting Begins*. New York: Free Press, 1994.

——. *Culture Wars*. New York: BasicBooks, 1991.

Kuhn, Thomas. *The Structure of Scientific Revolutions*. Chicago: University of Chicago Press, 1970.

Lindbeck, George. *The Nature of Doctrine: Religion and Theology in a Post-liberal Age*. Philadelphia: Westminster Press, 1984.

Lyotard, Jean-François. *The Postmodern Condition*. Translated by Geoff Bennington and

Brian Massumi. Minneapolis: University of Minnesota Press, 1984.

MacIntyre, Alasdair. *After Virtue.* Notre Dame, Ind.: University of Notre Dame Press, 1981

May, Gerald. *Addiction and Grace.* San Francisco: HarperCollins, 1988.

McCloskey, Donald N. *If You're So Smart: The Narrative of Economic Expertise.* Chicago: University of Chicago Press, 1990.

McKee, Robert. *Story.* New York: HarperCollins, 1997.

Middleton, J. Richard, and Brian J. Walsh. *Truth Is Stranger Than It Used to Be.* Downers Grove, Ill.: InterVarsity Press, 1995.

Milbank, John. *Theology and Social Theory: Beyond Secular Reason.* Oxford: Blackwell, 1990.

Newbigin, Lesslie. *Foolishness to the Greeks.* Grand Rapids, Mich.: Eerdmans, 1986.

———. *The Gospel in a Pluralist Society.* Grand Rapids, Mich.: Eerdmans, 1989.

———. *Proper Confidence: Faith, Doubt and Certainty in Christian Discipleship.* Grand Rapids, Mich.: Eerdmans, 1995.

Osborne, Grant. *The Hermeneutical Spiral.* Downers Grove, Ill.: InterVarsity Press, 1991.

Polanyi, Michael. *Science, Faith and Society.* Chicago: University of Chicago Press, 1964.

Ramachandra, Vinoth. *Gods That Fail: Modern Idolatry and Christian Mission.* Downers Grove, Ill.: InterVarsity Press, 1997.

———. *Recovery of Mission: Beyond the Pluralist Paradigm.* Grand Rapids, Mich.: Eerdmans, 1997.

Said, Edward. *Orientalism.* New York: Pantheon, 1978.

Taylor, Charles. *Sources of the Self: The Making of the Modern Identity.* Cambridge, Mass.. Harvard University Press, 1989.

Thistleton, Anthony. *Interpreting God and the Postmodern Self.* Grand Rapids, Mich.: Eerdmans, 1995.

Tilly, Terrence. *Postmodern Theologies: Challenges of Religious Diversity.* Maryknoll, N.Y.· Orbis, 1995.

Wright, N. T. *Jesus and the Victory of God.* Minneapolis: Fortress, 1996